HUNTED
BY THE KGB

Also by Sophie Berecz
In His Hands

HUNTED
BY THE KGB

The Theodor Pawluk Story

AS TOLD TO **SOPHIE BERECZ**

Pacific Press® Publishing Association
Nampa, Idaho
Oshawa, Ontario, Canada
www.pacificpress.com

Cover design by Lars Justinen
Cover illustration by Lars Justinen
Inside design by Steve Lanto

All scriptures are quoted from the King James Version.

Additional copies of this book are available by calling toll-free
1-800-765-6955 or online at www.adventistbookcenter.com.

Library of Congress Cataloging-in-Publication Data

Pawluk, Theodor, 1925-
Hunted by the KGB / Theodor Pawluk as told to Sophie Berecz.
        p. cm.
    ISBN-13: 978-0-8163-2257-2 (pbk.)
    ISBN-10: 0-8163-2257-0 (pbk.)
  1. Pawluk, Theodor, 1925- 2. Ukrainian Americans—Biography.
3. Seventh-day Adventists—Biography. 4. Pawluk, Theodor, 1925—Childhood
and youth. 5. World War, 1939-1945—Personal narratives, Ukrainian.
  6. Ukraine—History—German occupation, 1941-1944—Biography.
7. Ukraine—History—1944-1991—Biography. 8. Military deserters—Soviet
Union—Biography. 9. Soviet Union. Sovetskaia Armiia—Biography.
  10. Soviet Union. Komitet gosudarstvennoi bezopasnosti—History.
        I. Berecz, Sophie, 1973- II. Title.
            E184.U5P39 2008
            940.54'81477—dc22

                2007051135

08 09 10 11 12 • 5 4 3 2 1

Dedication

For Isabelle, Lucy, and baby Lydia.

Acknowledgments

Theodor

These are the people who have inspired me to share my life's story. My wife, Klara; our children and their spouses, Stephen and Carol Pawluk, Jan and Ellen Kaatz; our close church friends, Hasmik Melikian, Priscilla McNeily; and Ellen G. White.

> There are thousands of souls willing to work for the Master who have not had the privilege of hearing the truth as some have heard it, but they have been faithful readers of the Word of God, and they will be blessed in their humble efforts to impart light to others. Let such ones keep a diary, and when the Lord gives them an interesting experience, let them write it down, as Samuel did when the armies of Israel won a victory over the Philistines. He set up a monument of thankfulness, saying, "Hitherto hath the Lord helped us." Brethren, where are the monuments by which you keep in view the love and goodness of God?
> —Ellen G. White Comments, *SDA Bible Commentary*, vol. 2, p. 1012.

Sophie

Thank You, most of all, to God who enabled me to write amid the chaos of toddlers, diaper changes, and the joys of pregnancy. Thanks also to my mother, Martha Travis, for her invaluable support during the writing of this book and, as always, to my husband, Monty.

Contents

Chapter 1

The Soviet searchlight swept its beam, sharp and powerful, across the dark field, skimming over the top of the tall grass. The beam etched silhouettes of isolated trees into the night sky. Theodor Pawluk threw himself, for what seemed like the hundredth time, onto the ground. His frosty breath wisped upward in the winter air. He cringed as armored vehicles droned along the nearby road. The soft thumps and quickened breaths on each side of him told Theodor that his two companions had also hit the earth. Crawling on knees and elbows, the three fugitives inched their way through thick grass and weeds that covered this stretch of the Austrian border. In pitch darkness again, they stooped and ran until the spotlight once more circled and swept over them. Down, crawl. Up, run. Down, crawl. Through it all, the cold night air burned his lungs. He tried to think of nothing but the next step.

At first, Theodor felt exhilarated to be free from the Soviet army. On their flight from Budapest, Hungary, following the rumpled map that Theodor carried with him, the three deserters had trudged the country roads, avoiding all main thoroughfares and cities. The Soviet army occupied this Hungarian land, after all. Once across the Austrian border, there were yet more barriers to cross before reaching the American Sector in West Germany. If the Soviets caught them, it would be the end of Theodor's dream. And of him.

Though it was winter during their escape, Theodor, Petro, and Ivan* always spent their nights outdoors. In this region most farmers simply stored their hay in the fields. Waiting until dark, the three would crawl into a pile of hay and sleep there. In the morning, before anybody might spot them, the tired and dirty trio was up again and on their way.

When it came to food, Theodor and his companions lacked the cash, let alone the currencies of the countries through which they were fleeing, to buy provisions. So they ate whatever could be scavenged from the fields. Most days it was raw vegetables.

"The railroad track is just ahead," Ivan whispered over their muffled footsteps. From somewhere a curse answered. Theodor remembered surveying this plot of land in the daylight. The three, all Ukrainian defectors from the Soviet army, had arrived at the Austrian border on Saturday, after a week of running. Theodor, Petro, and Ivan had waited for the cover of darkness to conceal their crossing from the border patrol. There were no houses in this section of land, but an elevated track would expose them as they crossed it.

"Don't try it," some locals had warned. "Crossing that track is suicide. You'll be dead men."

"We'll make it," Theodor insisted. *If they only knew. God has always provided in the past,* he thought. *He will see me through this too.* The railroad was only one of the hurdles ahead of them that night, let alone on this journey. The sweep of the searchlights grew more frequent the closer the runaways crawled to the border. In the darkness Theodor breathed another ragged prayer for help. As he scuttled toward the exposed track, he recalled another border-crossing experience—his father's. *Now I know what he must have*

_____

* Petro and Ivan are pseudonyms.

felt, Theodor thought, his elbows grinding into the dirt. *How I miss him.* His father's tale was where it all had begun.

The searchlight plunged. Down, crawl. Up, run. Down, crawl.

——*—*

Young Onofre Pawluk squinted at the enemy line through his cover of undergrowth, sizing up the narrowing distance between forces. The Communist revolutionary force pressed toward him while the might and power of Tsar Nicholas II—the Russian army—inched forward at his side. Bullets sizzled through the autumn air. Onofre scrutinized his companions, like him covered with sweat, dirt, and fear. Like him, they each knew the secret. At the sound of gunfire, he tensed, alert, waiting. Freedom. There would be only one chance.

The Russian government, his current captor and commander, had promised freedom to these Austrian prisoners of war. "When you defeat the revolutionaries, you will be allowed to return to your country," Onofre recalled their pledge. His mind raced back to Galicia, his homeland in the Ukraine, bordered on the south by Romania and Hungary, on the west by Czechoslovakia, and on the north by the Polish-Russian border. With a population of only two thousand, Onofre's home village of Kornich, five kilometers from the city of Kolomeya, was small; but for his eighteen years, it had been the center of his world. Yet even the Ukraine wasn't entirely free. Before World War I, his country belonged to the Austrian crown.

That was why, in June 1914, the Austrian army had drafted Onofre to fight against the Russians. Not long into the war, the army of Tsar Nicholas II had captured Onofre's unit, hauling the prisoners of war to Vladivostok, Siberia. While he was in Siberian captivity in October of 1917, the month Onofre turned nineteen, the Bolshevik Revolution erupted in Russia. The tsar's army, under the direction of Admiral Aleksandr Kolchak, fought against the Communist revolutionary forces, who were led by General Leon Trotsky.

As the war intensified, the demand for manpower grew. Scores of Russian peasants joined the revolutionary ranks in the fight against the tsar's army and his government of oppression. The tsar's officials followed the suggestion to recruit Ukrainian prisoners of war, whose language was similar to the Russian language, and dangle the carrot of freedom before the prisoners, should they suppress the revolt. Onofre, along with thousands of other Ukrainians—serving as Austrian prisoners of war—played as a puppet now to the Russian army, fighting the Bolshevik uprising.

It was time. The enemy line was but a stone's toss away.

Hunkered on the front line, Onofre eyed the Russian tsar's officers commanding their stations. In a few minutes, he hoped he would be forever free of them and their hateful authority. Despite the lure of promised freedom in the Russian army, discontent in the Ukrainian-born Russian ranks had grown until life seemed unbearable. Onofre and his fellow soldiers plotted mutiny: deserting their posts and defecting to the other side en masse. This was the only way, they all agreed, to escape the army; there would be safety in numbers. They would wait for the opportunity, should it ever come.

Sweat beaded and trickled down Onofre's forehead. *Perhaps another conspirator will do the job,* he hoped. But no, he remembered, the burden of the task was all his. Onofre flexed his broad shoulders, clenching and unclenching his fists. He would wait for a turned head, a distracting grenade, or a slowdown in the barrage. His rifle lay beside him. There was a pause. Like a shot, he leaped, the crazed hope for freedom pounding in his chest, and raced for the enemy side.

"Pawluk is defecting!" he heard the shouts behind him. The tsar's officers opened fire. Bullets filled the air around him like a sandstorm, yet none of them touched Onofre. He crossed the battle lines and dropped, exhausted, to the ground.

I'm still alive! he marveled. *God must have protected me.* Onofre tucked his gratefulness into his heart to ponder later, for now revolutionary soldiers surrounded him, guns poised, waiting to hear what he had to say.

"There are several thousand soldiers from the Ukraine, former prisoners of war, wanting to come over," Onofre said, panting. He wiped the sweat from his face. "They suggested that I come over and ask you to stop shooting at them tomorrow." He tried to sound like he was asking for a casual favor. "That will be a sign for them to come over too. Do you need any more ammunition? Guns?" The revolutionists grinned. Hands pulled him up, thumping him on the shoulders.

The following day, thousands of former Austrian soldiers broke from the tsar's army and defected to the revolutionary army. They brought with them much of the military hardware that the Communists needed so desperately. It was a great victory for both Onofre and for the Communist revolt.

Overnight, Onofre became an important military hero and a friend of the Communist system. He was rewarded with a high-ranking position in the Communist army and, after the revolution, in the civil government. Given his leading role in the new order, Onofre also received a passport that enabled him to travel the entire Soviet Union without paying for transportation. For several years Onofre enjoyed high society life, but as time went on, the glamour lost its charm. He grew homesick for the place he was born—western Ukraine—homesick for his father and mother, his brothers and sisters, his friends. Life would not be easy anymore, but home was home.

After long and thoughtful planning, Onofre asked his superior for a vacation to go home to see his parents. Onofre was granted the leave, but he was encouraged to return to his employment in the Soviet Union. He never did. The summer of 1920, Onofre left Russia and returned to West Ukraine, which though free of Austrian rule was now under the dominion of the Polish government. Once Onofre reached home, he saw everything from a new perspective—his life was a gift. Three years later Onofre married

Hanoucy, in his hometown Greek Orthodox church. Now he had something to live for.

* * * *

So did his son. Now in the late autumn of 1945, the spotlight was on Theodor, trying to pin him and his two companions under its relentless sweep. A vision of his father crossing the front lines, formed from years of countless retelling, spurred Theodor to faith. As the men reached the railroad track, they waited for the searchlight to sweep past. Then, in a desperate plunge, the three leaped over the track and hit the ground just as another probe lit the air around them. Taking no more chances, the men inched forward through the field on elbows and knees for two painful hours.

At last, the Austrian side. Although farmhouse lights flickered invitingly in the "safety zone," the three fugitives knew better than to seek refuge in any home this close to the border. Spent from crawling, Theodor and his two friends remained in the field for the rest of the night. Burrowing into a large pile of hay, they stretched out to sleep.

Severe pain shot through Theodor's chest as he lay down. His muscles cramping from the crawling, Theodor winced. Afraid to complain to his friends about the pain, Theodor rolled onto his other side, clenching his teeth. *Thank You for Your protection, God,* he prayed instead, his heart full. Fragments of his former life flickered in erratic scenes across his mind; despite the hunger pangs and cramping muscles, sleep came quickly.

* * * *

Shortly after his marriage in 1923, Onofre Pawluk's interest in God and the church grew, especially when he reflected on his miraculous survival while changing sides between the tsar's and the revolutionary's armies. He began attending the Greek Orthodox services faithfully. Every day at 6:00 A.M., Onofre knelt for prayer at morning Mass. With such devotion, he was soon a leading member of the local church.

"Hanoucy," he announced one day to his wife. "I want to buy a Bible."

"What?" she said. "Isn't hearing the priest read the Bible every day enough?"

"Not anymore," he replied. "I want to own one for myself. Then I can read it any time I want."

"How are you going to get one?" Hanoucy asked.

"I don't know," Onofre said, frowning. "I don't think it's going to be easy. There's no place to buy a Bible around here, so I'll have to travel to the city. I know it will be an expensive purchase, but it's worth it to me."

"I've never heard of anyone except a priest owning a Bible. Will they even let you buy one?"

"That's the hard part. I'm going to have to get permission from our priest to study one. That makes me nervous."

"But he respects you," Hanoucy pointed out. "Maybe because of your high standing in the church, the priest will allow you to have one."

When Onofre gathered enough courage to ask the priest's permission, he found that Hanoucy was right: he was granted permission. After spending a small fortune on a Bible, Onofre delightedly opened the sacred pages for himself. Every evening after he finished the day's work, he pored over its pages.

"Listen to this, Hanoucy," he would say. "I have never heard this before." As Onofre turned each page, a whole new world opened before him. The Bible soon became his most precious possession.

On February 21, 1925, Theodor was born to the Pawluk family. By now his father, Onofre, was well thought of in the village, and the community celebrated Theodor's infant baptism in the Greek Orthodox church as a great event.

As Onofre continued to read his Bible, he was amazed at what he found in the Holy Scripture—things that he had never heard before: how God created our world in six days (Exodus 20:11), how sin entered our world (Genesis 3:1–7), how God saves the repentant sinner (John 3:16), how God will restore our world to how it was before sin (Revelation 21:1–5), and how it is a sin to worship idols and images (Exodus 20:3–6).

This latter discovery especially stumped him. In his house, on the wall that faced east, hung golden images and icons, pictures of the saints, a crucifix, and a large picture of the virgin Mary. He and his wife reverently knelt before them all every morning. When anyone in the family felt sick, Onofre or Hanoucy would dip a finger into their precious holy water and dab the sick person's forehead.

The holy water was scooped from the river every year on January 6, the Feast of Epiphany. The members of the Greek Orthodox church followed their priest in a procession to the nearest frozen river. Once there, they cut three crosses from the ice and decorated them in honor of Christ's birth. The priest blessed the crosses and the water below the ice. Following the blessing, the villagers made their way onto the frozen river. Braving the ice, they dipped little jars into the three holes, filling their containers to the brim with the precious icy liquid. Like the rest of the pious church members, Onofre and Hanoucy hung the jar on the wall and put flowers around it. Throughout the year, when someone in the home was sick or injured, a little dab of water applied to the forehead or wound was supposed to bring a cure.

One Sunday, Onofre again mustered his courage and approached the village priest with a question. "Why do we not follow the Bible's teaching in reference to image worship?"

"What do you mean?" asked the priest.

"The Bible says 'Thou shalt not make unto thee any graven image or any likeness of any thing that is in heaven above, or that is in the earth beneath, or that is in the water under the earth. Thou shalt not bow down thyself to them.'* Aren't we disobeying God's law?"

---

* Exodus 20:4, 5.

The priest paused. "You know, the rest of the church members are not as advanced in religious matters as you are," he said, dismissing Onofre's concern. "It would be impossible to make any changes right now. Don't let it trouble you, Onofre. We're not really praying to the images after all, just whom they represent."

"Oh," Onofre said, nodding. "I see." But he did not. *Shouldn't we pray only to God?* The conviction continued to gnaw at him. He continued to attend church, but Onofre's questions wouldn't go away.

"You know, Lutherans don't worship and pray to idols like the Greek Orthodox do," a friend mentioned one day. "Why don't you go visit them? There is a little church in Kolomeya."

Onofre set out the very next Sunday to attend the Lutheran church. He didn't simply want to talk with them; he wanted to witness their entire service. But if word got out that he was visiting another church, Onofre knew the priest would be angry, especially since Onofre was a leader in the congregation. *I'll just go to check it out one time,* Onofre rationalized.

Not knowing what to expect, Onofre sat in the back row of the small church. Here there were no pictures of saints, no images, and no chanting—nothing he was accustomed to—just reading and interpreting the Holy Scriptures. Onofre loved it. Intrigued by this new theology and worship style, he returned by himself week after week. After meeting with the Lutherans several Sundays, Onofre could no longer keep this experience to himself.

"Please come to our house next Sunday and share your message with my family and neighbors," he asked the Lutheran minister. Word soon trickled throughout Kornich, Onofre's small village, and news of Onofre's invitation reached the priest.

When the priest learned that there was to be a religious meeting in Onofre's home, he devised a plan. Gathering all the worshipers attending his church that Sunday, the priest called them to follow him in a big crusade to the Pawluk house. "We must put a stop to those Lutheran meetings," he cried, "before they deceive anyone else." The parishioners eagerly followed their priest out the door of the church and down the road. As they marched, more and more people joined the raucous crowd. Surrounding the house, they yelled and threatened. Emboldened by the priest, the rioters knocked on the door and shouted at the windows, ready to turn the house upside down if they could.

"Open the door, Pawluk." Onofre recognized the threatening voice of a fellow leader of the church. "We know what you're trying to do. You can't get away from us. We will have no heresy taught in our village. We'll show you what God says about people like you. Let us in now!" Onofre and Hanoucy, the Lutheran minister, and the tiny congregation waited in silence. The pounding continued. "Open the door!"

Onofre refused.

"Don't trouble yourself, Pawluk," someone yelled. "We'll open it for you." Hanoucy clutched little Theodor tightly. After several men kicked and smashed the door off its hinges, the mob surged inside.

Chapter 2

Theodor awoke with a start. The hay scratched his skin. He pushed an opening in the sheltering haystack while the early morning light flooded his still-sleepy eyes. Taking a deep breath of the cold air, Theodor surveyed the brown Austrian fields stretching around him. Mercifully, throughout the escape, the weather had remained temperate. No rain, no snow. *Thank You, Lord,* he prayed silently.

Theodor's chest pains were gone. His stomach, however, churned for food. What would it be today? A rancid radish, a tasteless cucumber, wilted cabbage? It didn't matter. There wasn't going to be any breakfast. He tucked in his shirt, now hanging loosely over his hunger-ravaged frame, and wrapped himself again in his long coat. His once-solid body now weighed about one hundred thirty-five pounds.

The stubbly field extended to a nearby country road. Though the surrounding countryside was dotted with farmhouses, they dared not slow down to beg or scrounge for food. Despite crossing the border, they were still in Russian-occupied territory. There was simply no way to get something to eat.

Theodor and his two friends brushed themselves off and started to walk again. Now into the second week of their journey, they were pushing on toward Vienna. Another barrier, the Danube River, lay in front of them. The only bridge where they could cross the large river lay in Vienna.

As they had through Romania and Hungary, the travelers trudged for several days through Austria on small rural roads, stopping only to sleep in more piles of hay. Across forests, farmlands, and pastureland they hiked, spying only the occasional farmer and wagon.

By now it was all the men could do to keep walking. In Europe, every kilometer was marked by a wooden post. Theodor would walk for one kilometer and then rest at the wooden post. Another kilometer, another rest. Endlessly it dragged on. Once in sheer exhaustion, Theodor bowed his head in prayer. The older of his companions, Petro, eyed him with scorn. "You're not making it any easier for us," the man said, snorting. He turned his tall, bony frame away in disgust.

"Maybe we should try to get a ride to Vienna," Ivan suggested.

"We'll have to cross over to the main highway," said Petro, his face red from windburn. "They still could be looking for us."

"It's worth a risk," returned Ivan. "Let's see your map again, Theodor."

Theodor took out the wrinkled map from his coat pocket, opening it on the ubiquitous wooden kilometer post. "From this map, we've still got a long way to go," Ivan said, tracing his finger over their route. "We won't get to safety anytime soon at the rate we're going, stopping every kilometer like this."

"Alright," said Theodor. "Let's try it."

"If the Russians spot us, there'll be no place to hide," Petro added. "Your prayers won't do you any good." He spat on the ground. Theodor ignored Petro as he folded the map. Ivan was already up and crossing the field toward the distant highway. Theodor and Petro caught up to him and then, once on the main road, the three began to hitchhike. Not much later, and to their great surprise, a large truck with an open bed started slowing down for the bedraggled hitchhikers.

"There'll be plenty of room for all three of us," Theodor said, relieved. As the truck pulled over in front of them, two Russian army soldiers—dressed in all-too-familiar drab green uniforms, red stars on their caps—nodded at them from the cab. Theodor felt as if a snake had bitten him. Petro swore under his breath. Theodor stilled his pounding heart and tried to look composed. A glance at his companions told him that they, too, were trying to look unruffled. It was unthinkable now to decline the ride, and sizing up the rifle the passenger soldier carried, Theodor knew it was pointless to run.

"Thanks!" Theodor waved. Petro and Ivan nodded and smiled sheepishly. All three climbed into the bed of the truck. The truck geared back up and headed down the road. As the countryside rushed by, Theodor felt sick. *Now what?* he wondered.

"Great idea," growled Petro in a low tone, glaring at the others. "We caught a ride all right. Or rather, it caught us."

"Be quiet," snapped Ivan, "and act cheerful."

"I'm happy, I'm happy," snarled Petro. He pasted on a grin and glanced at the rear window of the cab.

Maybe they don't suspect anything, Theodor hoped, stretching out his sore legs.

"Good thing we got rid of that lovely Russian *kubanka* you were wearing," said Ivan to Theodor. His friends had insisted Theodor get rid of that warm wool military hat. Walking across a field after their first escape, they had met a lone Romanian man. Negotiating a cap swap, they placed Theodor's *kubanka* on the man's head. The man was pleased, for it was a warm hat, but Theodor hated to part with it.

The trio's clothing, though simple and warm, betrayed the truth: they wore their rumpled attire night and day alike. Luckily, the Soviet army had not yet given the men their military uniforms. It would have been difficult to get rid of three military uniforms and find civilian garb for the three of them, especially when they had no money. Despite their civilian clothes, Theodor knew they didn't totally blend in.

"Maybe they haven't suspected anything," said Ivan.

"Oh yeah," said Petro. "Three beat-up, skinny men near the Hungarian border, hitchhiking. They're bound to be curious, and that means one thing." The man narrowed his eyes. "They're not going to let us go without finding out."

"They can't hear us back here, but they're watching us from the rear window," reported Ivan. Theodor couldn't resist the urge to turn his head casually and check.

"You're right. It doesn't look good." Listening to the roar of the engine and the incessant rattling of the truck bed, the men slumped against the sides, staring at the blurring, brown landscape.

"OK," Theodor said. "We have roughly two hours to plan how to get out of this mess. We can't jump out now without serious injury. Any ideas?"

"Plan A: we can ask to be dropped off when we come to Vienna," said Ivan.

"Very funny," snorted Petro. "Plan B?"

"We're going to have to jump out."

"And hike the rest of the way on broken legs. I'm in," Petro muttered.

"They've got to slow down somewhere in the city because of all the pedestrians," Theodor said. "We've just got to be ready to leap the instant they brake."

Two hours passed by as the men planned their latest escape. While they talked, the soldier in the passenger seat kept a sharp eye on them. Theodor spent much of the time they weren't talking with his head down in silent prayer. Every time he bowed his head, Petro spat in contempt. Theodor pretended not to notice.

Protected from the wind by the sides of the truck bed, the men tried to keep cheerful. The sun warmed their shoulders, the landscape was new, and the longed-for city grew closer by the minute. Best of all, they could rest. At times, his eyes closed and his head resting on the vibrating truck side, Theodor could almost imagine feeling that all was as it used to be before the war. Maybe they were worried for nothing.

It was midmorning when they reached Vienna. Plan A. When Ivan crawled over to knock on the rear window, the soldiers in the cab ignored them. Instead, the driver picked up speed so that they could not jump off.

"Looks like they are taking us to their headquarters to be investigated," Petro said. "We're in big trouble."

"Watch for a place to jump out," Ivan replied. "Surely they'll have to slow down sometime."

Theodor didn't say anything. His head was bowed, and he was praying. Petro scowled.

The truck continued its high speed. "We're passing Vienna," Petro's voice surged with desperation. "We've got to jump out."

"Hold on," Theodor whispered. On the outskirts of the city, Theodor spotted the flag at the entrance to the Soviet headquarters just ahead.

"Oh no," yelped Ivan.

"Get ready," Petro warned.

A few yards from the entrance, the truck slowed. "Now!" Theodor ordered in a whisper. Out they leaped from the truck bed, their knees nearly buckling from the force of the impact. But they kept going, disappearing among the people thronging the city sidewalks. Hearing shouts from behind, the three kept a casual pace, trying to look inconspicuous. After zigzagging some distance on the busy city streets, they wove their way back to the city center. Theodor breathed a silent prayer of thanks to God for His deliverance.

The sun was almost overhead when the escapees reentered Vienna. With plenty of time still to walk around the city, they found themselves in the American section of Vienna. What a relief it was for Theodor to see American soldiers rather than the dreaded Soviets. Continuing to walk, they found an American train departing the city.

"Is there any chance we could get on this train and get out of the Russian-occupied area?" they asked the American soldiers stationed there.

"Of course," the Americans replied, "but the Russians will search this train as it leaves Vienna. Still interested?" Theodor and his friends discussed this option.

The Russians are sure to find us on the train. Isn't there some place we could stow away? they wondered. No. After exhausting all possibilities for getting out of the Russian-occupied area by train, the discouraged trio returned to the original plan of walking. They returned downtown. As they trudged block after city block, evening slowly wrapped itself around Vienna. Cheerful glimmers from the buildings all around twinkled, torturing them with visions of safety and comfort.

As Theodor tramped through the darkened city, a fleeting look through the window of one home sent a pang of nostalgia through him. A family sat, cozy around a white covered table, enjoying their meal. Theodor remembered his mother setting out the white Sabbath tablecloth every Friday evening. He could almost taste the steaming vegetables, fresh bread, beans, polenta, and delicious pierogi that she piled on the table while he and his brothers and sister sat around it, waiting expectantly. He could see again his father picking up his Bible, the friendly banter of the children quieting. After Father read a passage from Scripture, the family would sing one Sabbath song together. Father would pray, and then the whole family would devour the meal. Theodor treasured those Friday evenings, sitting with his brothers and sister around the fireplace while Father told stories of how God had led and protected them in the past. A weaver by trade, Theodor's father spent hours on his loom, crafting beautiful fabric. Around the hearth at home it was no different. With the same deft skill, his father wove stories of faith tightly into the fabric of young Theodor's heart.

* — * — * — *

It was 1926. As the angry mob crashed through the splintered door, filling the Pawluk living room, a woman attending the Lutheran service screamed. Baby Theodor, not yet a year old, started to cry. Hanoucy quickly placed him in his father's arms, hoping to deter the villagers from attacking Onofre. Onofre's family and friends waited for the worst, their eyes wide and faces white. All of them prayed, as more and more rioters squeezed inside the small space. In the chaos, one of the Greek Orthodox church leaders stepped up to Onofre. "We are doing this for God," he shouted. "We will not let this heretic corrupt this town," he continued, waving at the Lutheran pastor. Pointing right at Onofre, he narrowed his eyes. "You will go to hell for this."

Onofre, holding tightly to his son, stared at the man. The speaker, a faithful and devout leader in the church, never had behaved like this before. Furious with righteous indignation, Onofre's accuser stepped to the table where the Lutheran minister stood and struck the preacher in the face.

The minister reeled, and his face grimaced in pain. Still, he remained calm. Taking a deep breath, he looked directly at his attacker. "The Bible says that 'whosoever shall smite thee on thy right cheek, turn to him the other also.' "* He turned his head. "Here is my other cheek."

The man stared at the minister, stunned. He had never heard anyone talk that way. His face grew red with embarrassment. Suddenly ashamed of his action, the leader slowly backed through the crowd toward the broken door, then walked out of the house.

"What happened?" the people outside clamored. "Why are you leaving? What's wrong?" He repeated to them the scripture that the minister quoted. The people closest to him reported the verse to those behind them. With a rippling effect, the Bible quotation sank like an anchor of restraint through the turbulent crowd. As quickly as they had invaded Onofre's property, the mob now melted away.

That was the last day of Onofre's membership in the Greek Orthodox Church. After the confrontation at the Pawluk farm, the priest promptly excommunicated Onofre forever, condemning him

---

* Matthew 5:39.

as a heretic. The villagers cooperated by rejecting the entire family. They refused to speak with Onofre or to do business with him. Even Onofre's parents, extended family, and friends rejected them. Onofre's customers for his small weaving trade started taking their business elsewhere. Apart from their immediate family and the Lutheran church members, the Pawluks' social network vanished.

In time, however, Onofre won back his customers. While his competitors often appropriated leftover thread or yarn for themselves when they finished a job, Onofre could be trusted to return every ounce of thread back to the customer. People valued his integrity, and it was not long before his business rebounded.

In June of 1927, baby Slawko was born. Because Onofre had been excommunicated from the church, Slawko, unlike his older brother, Theodor, never received infant baptism.

Onofre continued attending the Lutheran church and, impressed with their teachings that followed the Bible, became a Lutheran too. He attended church faithfully and participated in as many church activities as he could, even traveling to various Lutheran conventions throughout the country. In spite of all these blessings and his delight in his new church, Onofre's greatest joy was studying the Holy Scripture for himself.

One day, as he read the Bible, he found this startling passage.

> Remember the sabbath day, to keep it holy. Six days shalt thou labour, and do all thy work: But the seventh day is the sabbath of the LORD thy God: in it thou shalt not do any work, thou, nor thy son, nor thy daughter, thy manservant, nor thy maidservant, nor thy cattle, nor thy stranger that is within thy gates: For in six days the LORD made heaven and earth, the sea, and all that in them is, and rested the seventh day: wherefore the LORD blessed the sabbath day, and hallowed it.*

---

* Exodus 20:8–11.

In English Bible translations, the commandment says, "Remember the *Sabbath* to keep it holy." In Russian, Ukrainian, Polish, and other Slovak languages, the fourth commandment does not say the *Sabbath* day. It reads, "Remember Saturday *[Subota]* to keep it holy." For Onofre, there was no question which day was the Sabbath. He continued searching the Bible for further enlightenment. The more he studied, the more surprised he grew.

Why have I never heard anyone preach, or even mention, the seventh-day Sabbath before? he wondered. *Isn't the Bible clear on the Sabbath subject?* Nowhere could he find that it had been changed. After reading the Bible cover to cover, Onofre remained convinced. To him, the Bible stated the Sabbath commandment plainly, and he would not compromise. With enthusiasm, Onofre started sharing his findings with everyone who would listen.

"No, no," his Lutheran friends argued, "the Sabbath is no longer significant. It belongs to the Old Testament, which was for the Jews only. We are living under a new covenant now. In the New Testament, we observe the Sabbath on Sunday because Jesus was resurrected on Sunday." No matter how many times Onofre shared with them about the seventh-day Sabbath, discussing the reasons he still found the commandment valid, his Lutheran friends could not see the light he had found. To Onofre, however, keeping the day God ordained as holy was not a matter he could compromise. He determined to learn everything possible about the seventh-day Sabbath. He did not care what others thought about the biblical truth he had just discovered.

Not far from Theodor's home lived a Jewish store owner. As the Jews were the only people in his area who observed the biblical Sabbath, Onofre decided to pay him a visit. "How do you keep the Sabbath holy?" he asked. "When does it begin?"

"The Sabbath starts at sundown on Friday," the shopkeeper explained.

"Not at midnight like Sunday observance?" Onofre asked, surprised. "And when does it end?"

"At sundown on Saturday night." The Jewish man went on to describe other traditions his family observed. After hearing all these details, Onofre made up his mind that, even if it meant worshiping alone, he and his family would observe the Sabbath according to the Bible. With the sun slipping down behind the horizon, the following Friday Onofre and his family celebrated the coming Sabbath, welcoming its peace into their home.

As Onofre continued to study his Bible, another conviction grew—smoking tobacco was not part of God's plan for human beings. Though Onofre had smoked heavily since his youth, he decided to quit. Despite fervent prayers, however, his resolve lasted only as long as the need for the next cigarette. Quitting seemed impossible.

One day while plowing his field, the desire to overcome nicotine addiction overwhelmed Onofre. "Lord," he prayed, bowing his head, "please strike me dead if I ever put another cigarette in my mouth." With that, he took out his tobacco package, dropped it in the field, and plowed over the entire package, burying it in the soft earth.

Later that day, as Onofre sat working at his loom, a customer entered the room. A foul odor accompanied the man. "You must have stepped into some dog dung in our courtyard," he told the man. "Can you please check your shoes?"

The customer examined both shoes. "No, there's nothing on them," the man replied. "I don't smell anything."

Following a short conversation, the customer pulled out his tobacco pouch. "Want one?" he asked, offering Onofre a cigarette.

"No thanks," Onofre replied. As the customer opened his tobacco pouch, the putrid odor intensified. Onofre suddenly realized that the Lord had answered his prayer, replacing the formerly sweet, intoxicating smell with a revolting one. He never longed for tobacco again.

Onofre continued his fervent study of the Bible, seeking to surrender his life entirely to God. He hungered for the truths revealed in God's Word. "Ask and it will be given you," he read. "Seek, and ye shall find; knock, and it shall be opened unto you. For every one who asketh receiveth. And he that seeketh findeth, and to him that knocketh it shall be opened."* *What door will God open next?* he wondered.

It was his neighbor's. One day a man named Veretka, a Seventh-day Adventist colporteur from the city of Ivano-Frankovsk, two hundred kilometers away, came to Onofre's village selling books. The colporteur knew nothing of Onofre and his search for the true church. Onofre's family was not at home, so the colporteur stopped at the neighbor's place. Knowing Onofre's interest in religion, the neighbor bought one small book. The following day the neighbor brought it to Onofre, who gladly paid his unusually kind neighbor and began reading. He was thrilled to find that the book contained theological answers to many of the questions that plagued him.

Onofre flew through the book, devouring its pages. "Please send someone to visit my family," he wrote to the book's editor. "We'd like more information about the church you represent." A few weeks later, Onofre had his answer: someone was on the way. Onofre, Hanoucy, and the little children waited anxiously for the visit.

A Seventh-day Adventist pastor finally arrived and spent a week with the Pawluks, responding to the barrage of questions from the eager family. That week ended Onofre's search for the true church. When the time came for the pastor to leave, Onofre asked him for baptism. In the summer of 1928, Onofre emerged from the waters of the Prut River into membership in the Seventh-day Adventist Church. The pastor promised to visit regularly and often.

Onofre was soon sharing the marvelous message with others, beginning with his customers. The weaving business presented Onofre a great witnessing opportunity, and many a client heard from Onofre the joy of his new theology and of his love for Jesus.

---

* Matthew 7:7, 8.

It was not long before Sabbath-keeping groups of believers were studying the Bible with Onofre in four separate villages: Kornich, Huculivka, Kaminky, and White-Oslave. Each small church was fifteen to twenty kilometers apart, some tucked into the forest of the Carpathian Mountains. Without roads connecting them, Onofre usually hiked the miles on foot.

In June of 1929, Theodor's sister, Daria, was born. The boys were thrilled to have a little sister. When little Daria was only ten months old, however, a terrible sadness swept over the family—Hanoucy, after a lingering illness, died in 1930, not quite twenty-six years old. Slawko was almost three, and Theodor was five.

"God is punishing you for leaving the Orthodox Church," people callously told the grieving husband and father. "Her death is all your fault."

"No, Hanoucy Pawluk cannot be buried in the village cemetery," the priest announced to the mourning family. "She is a heretic."

"Wait," a villager protested. "Maybe she is still on the church books.

"Besides, it's not her fault her husband turned away. Maybe Onofre is the only one who was excommunicated. Let's check and see." Sure enough, Hanoucy's name was still there, clearing the way for her burial in the cemetery.

When the funeral procession bearing Hanoucy's coffin reached the entrance to the church, the determined priest stepped out of the doorway, blocking the entrance. He held up his hand.

"Either Onofre Pawluk goes in and I will stay outside," the priest relayed, "or he stays outside and I go in. There is not enough room inside the church for both of us."

Onofre deferred, remaining outside while the priest presided over the funeral of his dear wife.

Who will take care of the children now? the townspeople wondered. *There's no way Onofre can take care of them and his farm and business by himself.*

Onofre struggled to care for his three small children alone. The task was overwhelming. Though Adventist church members pitched in as much as they could, Onofre needed domestic help and fast.

By this time the Seventh-day Adventist denomination had sent Onofre's four fledgling churches a full-time pastor. Pastor Felte, a German, noticed the Pawluk family's difficult circumstances.

"I know a nice, single Seventh-day Adventist woman who once wanted to be a missionary," he offered. "She would be a very good mother for the children."

"Oh?" replied Onofre, his curiosity piqued. "Do you have her address?" Soon he and the young woman, Caroline, were writing and exchanging photos. Raised an Adventist, Caroline came from a Ukrainian settlement of Hussites, followers of the Reformer John Huss. In 1932, she traveled from a distant corner of the Ukraine to meet Onofre. With one look at Caroline, Onofre was smitten. She was everything he hoped for, and he praised God for sending the right woman into his life. Onofre and Caroline soon married.

From the start, Caroline's courage and resolve brightened the lives of the little home. Her tenacity to endure the prejudice and scorn from her new community, her patience at rearing three small children, her knowledge of Scripture, and her devotion to God and family were a well of encouragement to Onofre. Caroline took her new role seriously, never uttering complaint despite the icy treatment from her neighbors.

"She is a Seventh-day Adventist, after all," they gossiped. Since the villagers shunned her, Caroline could not ask any of them for help. The town people continually looked for ways to share their disapproval and make life unpleasant for Caroline. They were rude to her when she shopped in the market or when she passed them in the streets. Caroline's dependence on God strengthened her faith, and through experiencing persecution herself, she modeled to her children a character worth imitating. The Lord blessed the new marriage, and Theodor, Slawko, and Daria all quickly learned to love and respect their new mother.

As Theodor grew older, he traveled along with his father to the small mountain churches. It was fun to walk these long distances when people were eager to hear the message. After hiking so far, Theodor and his father usually stayed with the believers all day long. They held two lengthy meetings, with the shortest sermon lasting at least one hour. Not all the congregations had buildings in which to meet, and when the weather was warm and dry, Onofre led out services in the open fields surrounded by the beauty of wildflowers and forests.* Theodor enjoyed these trips to the little mountain churches, meeting the many young people his age who attended. As a bonus, the people in those villages never harassed them.

Little could Theodor know that many of these enthusiastic converts would someday be sent to Siberia or killed by the coming Communist regime. For now, under the new democracy, churches prospered all over the country.

In contrast, Theodor dreaded the weekly walks to his home church in Kolomeya. Villagers who saw the family often harassed the Pawluks, calling them all sorts of vile names and encouraging the town children to throw stones at Theodor and his family.

"Where are you going all dressed up, Theodor?" snickered the older village boys one Sabbath. Theodor was now old enough to walk alone. "It's Saturday. Don't you have some work to do?" a boy teased. Theodor smiled but didn't say anything. He kept walking, looking straight ahead. The older boy glowered at Theodor as he passed by.

"You touched me!" the boy accused, yelling, stopping in the road.

"I did?" replied Theodor, turning around.

"You touched me with your elbow. Why you filthy mutt!"

"No, I didn't," Theodor defended himself. "I'm sorry if I . . ." A brutal blow sent him reeling. "Take that," the bully yelled, hitting

---

* Today these churches are large and still growing. They now require large buildings to house the congregations.

him in his face so hard that the blow knocked out one of Theodor's teeth. Theodor was still bleeding when he arrived at church. Such abuse was common for Theodor. It was of no use to complain to the authorities. The community always sided against the "heretic" Pawluks.

But despite the hardships, the Pawluk family's life was filled with love and joy. The highlights of those times were those Friday evenings when the family gathered around the table.

*　*　*　*

On the cold streets of Vienna, the fleeting glimpses of the food and warmth brought tears to his eyes as he remembered happy family gatherings around the dinner table. Only four months earlier, his family had been banished to Siberia. *Here I am,* Theodor thought, *a fugitive in a foreign land, surrounded by enemies on every side. When the Soviets catch me, a deserter from their army, they will execute me on the spot. Then again, that will end my hardship,* he tried to reassure himself. *How I wish that Jesus would come right now to end this hostile world and set up His kingdom.* He wiped away the tears chilling his cheeks. *I've had enough.*

Late in the evening, Theodor and his friends stood at a busy intersection in Vienna, uncertain of where to turn. Just then, a troop of Russian soldiers, loaded guns slung over their shoulders, swarmed the sidewalks. "Time to go home," they threatened the passersby. "It's almost curfew. Everyone must be off the streets." Heads down, the three runaways picked up their pace, pretending to obey. They had too far to go to leave the city limits before curfew. But refusing the Russians' orders meant sure capture, interrogation, and death. They had no place to go.

Chapter 3

"Ten o'clock curfew!" barked a passing soldier on horseback. A horn blew from a nearby army truck. "Off the streets, now!"

On the corner, trapped in growing darkness, the enemy all around him, Theodor was lost and helpless. *Where can we go?* he wondered. The shoulders of his two friends sagged in discouragement. Because Petro did not like to see him praying, Theodor stepped a few paces away from them and bowed his head.

Father in heaven, he prayed desperately, *we need a place to stay. Please show us where to go. Thank You.* No sooner had he finished praying than a young Austrian man approached them.

"You can't stand here," the man said. "Are you looking for a place to stay overnight?"

"Yes," Theodor answered. "But I don't know where to go."

"Come. Follow me," the stranger said, "and I will show you a place where you'll be safe."

"Great!" Theodor replied, considering this invitation an answer to his prayers. He began to follow the man immediately. When Petro and Ivan stood unmoving, Theodor looked back and beckoned. "Come on," he urged them, lowering his voice. "It's OK." Petro frowned. Ivan shook his head, but took a step forward. Petro continued to resist, his expression revealing a mixture of stubbornness, anger, and fear. "There's no other choice," Theodor heard Ivan whisper to Petro.

"Curfew. Ten o'clock," a Russian soldier marched by again. Too close for comfort. Petro trailed far behind Theodor and Ivan.

The stranger led them through a maze of dark streets to a bombed-out apartment with few windows. "You can stay here all night," the man said. "Just walk in. This place is empty. You can sleep on the floor, and it will be warm. No one will bother you here." Theodor glimpsed a smile in the darkness, and then the man was gone as suddenly as he had come.

"How did you know that man was trustworthy?" asked Ivan, shaking his head. "No one would stop to help complete strangers like us with nothing to offer."

"I prayed for help, that's all," Theodor said.

"Oh," said Ivan, his voice thoughtful. A hiss was Petro's only reply.

Before stretching out in a corner to sleep, Theodor bowed his head. *Thank You, Father, for Your help once again.* Despite the hunger, narrow escape, and the ever-unknown future, Theodor's heart was an island of peace. He remembered his childhood school days: back then, the disapproval wasn't for praying, but for *not* praying.

＊—＊—＊—＊

"Everyone please stand for prayer," the teacher directed the class. It was the first day of school, and seven-year-old Theodor stood up obediently. "Our Father, which art in heaven," the class chanted in unison. "Hallowed be Thy name." Theodor did not mind repeating the Lord's Prayer. But the next request made him squirm.

"Now to mother Mary." Theodor's eyes widened in surprise.

"Hail Mary, full of grace," the teacher led. Theodor kept his mouth closed. Throughout the prayer, he remained silent, avoiding eye contact with his teacher.

Theodor remembered the many pictures of the saints, including the virgin Mary, that had once hung on the walls of their home. As

Theodor learned more about the Bible from Sabbath School and at home, he realized why his father no longer worshiped the icons. The painted wooden images had gradually become but mere decorations to Theodor too.

Then one day, his father took all the icons off the wall and carried them out to the barn. "Help me, Theodor," his father had said. "We are going to burn these images and pictures here in the barn so our neighbors will not see us. Let's clean this floor area well." Theodor helped his father pile the icons, beautiful and expensive, into a heap in the middle of the barn. "We must pray only to God," Onofre told his son as he lit the match.

"Don't follow me blindly," his father continued. "When you go to school, learn everything you can. Then make your own decisions. But we will no longer have these idols in our house."

Surrounded by other children reciting the prayer to Mary in the classroom, Theodor kept his mouth shut and tried to be invisible. Maybe the teacher wouldn't notice.

"Theodor Pawluk," the teacher ordered. Theodor winced. "Come forward, please." He reluctantly left his desk and walked to the front of the room. His classmates twittered behind him. "Hold out both your hands." Theodor did. "This is because you refuse to pray to mother Mary," she said. With that she struck his palms twice with her stinging rod. Tears rushed to Theodor's eyes, but he didn't cry. No matter what she said or did to him, he would pray only to God.

"Your teacher must think she is doing God a favor by punishing you," his father explained when Theodor returned home that first day. "She thinks you are a heretic, but you are following what God has asked you to do. Let me show you what God says." Onofre drew his son close and reached for the family Bible.

"About me?" asked Theodor.

"Yes, about you. 'Blessed are ye, when men shall revile you, and persecute you, and shall say all manner of evil against you falsely for my sake. Rejoice, and be exceeding glad: for great is your reward in heaven,' "* his father read. "I'm proud of you, Theo. This will probably happen again. Can you be brave?"

"Yes," answered young Theodor, the quiver in his voice belying his brave response.

Under the Polish government, the Ukrainians did not have any private church schools. Controlled by both the government and the Greek Orthodox Church, the schools enforced mandatory religion classes. Twice every week the village priest taught the children a class on the Orthodox religion. At the close of class, the priest herded the students to the nearby chapel. Each child knelt in a small booth, wracking his or her memory for mistakes to confess to the priest who was waiting behind a curtain. If the children's memory failed, the priest prompted them.

"Did you disobey your father today? Were you rude to your mother?"

Theodor squirmed. Though it seemed foolish to him, he couldn't get out of the ritual. Every day, if he confessed at all, he had to confess that he had disobeyed his teacher at prayer time, or worse, he had to confess that he was angry at the teacher for punishing him or that he was mad at the other kids for laughing at him. Usually he just said nothing, mutely waiting for the misery to end. Yet, as much as he dreaded the confessional booth, he loathed the forced prayer in class even more. Daily, for seven years, young Theodor refused to pray to Mary, and daily the teacher called him to the front. The sting on his hands, the jokes of his classmates, simply became a way of life.

——————*———*

Theodor, Ivan, and Petro awoke to the early morning bustle of people traveling on the street outside. The barren walls and hallways of the abandoned apartment building seemed to echo as loudly as their stomachs. "We've got to cross the bridge over the Danube

---

* Matthew 5:11, 12.

today," Ivan and Theodor agreed. "Then we'll see what we can find to eat." Petro eventually sat up from his corner, but wouldn't join them.

"Once we get our bearings, we'll head for the bridge first thing," Theodor said.

"You know there will be soldiers guarding the bridge, and they might be watching for us," Ivan surmised. "How are we going to get past them?"

"I don't know," Theodor said. "We'll think about that when the time comes." Petro groaned. Theodor looked at Petro, who sat with his head in his hands.

"There is no other way," said Theodor. "Let's go." Petro didn't move.

Ivan and Theodor led the way out of the apartment. Standing on the street corner, they turned and waited for Petro. When he finally stumbled out, they realized that something was very wrong. Petro's face was white, his eyes red. "I want to go home."

Alarmed, Theodor and Ivan rushed over to him.

"It's OK," Theodor encouraged their older friend. "Come on. We're going home. It just takes a while." He gently tugged on Petro's arm.

"We're going to make it," Ivan urged him too.

"No, no, no," Petro said, his voice revealing his anguish. "I can't do this anymore." He sat down on the street curb and sobbed bitterly. "I want to go home. I just want to go home."

"We *are* going home," Theodor soothed. "Look how far we've come, Petro. You can't stay here, or they will catch you. Just over the bridge, we're going to find something to eat, and you'll feel better. Come on."

Petro just cried louder. "I want to go home. I want to go home."

Theodor and Ivan looked at each other in dismay. People stopped, staring at the man. A small crowd gathered.

"Is everything OK?" a businessman asked. Petro sobbed into his hands, uncomprehending.

Theodor and Ivan coaxed and reasoned. "Please, Petro. Let's go. We'll just walk a little bit, and then we'll take a break. We'll find something to eat, and you can rest a while. Just get up, OK?" His two friends tried to help him to his feet. Petro pulled away, his hands shaking, his eyes wild and wet with tears.

"I want to go home."

It was no use. In a total mental collapse, Petro didn't have the capacity to understand.

"Send for a policeman," a bystander suggested. "This man needs help." Someone ran off to find one. *We have to leave before the police get here,* Theodor thought. He signaled to Ivan that they needed to leave. Ivan nodded back.

"Petro," said Theodor, his hand gently resting on his inconsolable companion. "We have to go now. We're so sad to say good-bye, but we have to keep going." Petro had traveled nearly two weeks with them and, despite his scorn for Theodor's prayers, had offered many good suggestions. How could they leave him now? Hearing an approaching policeman on horseback, Theodor gave Petro a final squeeze on his shoulder. Theodor and Ivan left Petro on the curb, surrounded by onlookers, and they hurried down the street.

With sorrowful hearts, the two friends headed toward the bridge at the outskirts of the city. A few hours of walking, mostly in silence, brought them to the massive bridge arching over the Danube River, an expanse too dangerous to swim. Studying the bridge, Theodor and Ivan groaned. Six Soviet military policemen stood guard at the entrance to the bridge—three on each side. All the travelers going by must stop and show their passports.

"They're looking for someone," whispered Theodor. "Probably us."

"The soldiers in the truck must have reported us," answered Ivan.

"We have to cross the river here," insisted Theodor. "There's no other way."

"But we have no passports, and they're stopping everyone."

"Just act confident. They might not notice us."

"Alright. Start praying," whispered Ivan. "Let's go."

At the busy entrance, Ivan walked ahead, his eyes averted. Theodor followed. Surrounded by the wagons, horses, and people pushing carts or carrying bundles, the two men stayed to the middle of the road. After they had passed the Russian military police and had started up the sloping bridge, a commotion among the police made Theodor's heart pound. He heard one of the three soldiers calling out from behind. "Run and check on those two. See who they are."

"God, help us!" Theodor prayed out loud. Although feeling panic, he forced his legs to keep a steady pace.

"Never mind," he heard the same officer call a few seconds later. "Come on back. Let them go." Incredulous, tears filled Theodor's eyes as he poured out his thanks to God for His intervention. " 'Call upon me in the day of trouble: I will deliver thee, and thou shalt glorify me,' "* he quoted quietly, remembering the passage he had memorized from the small, worn Bible tucked in his shirt.

"What just happened?" Ivan asked, as he evened his pace beside Theodor. "Was it your prayer again?"

"God is good," Theodor whispered. Ivan nodded. The two men kept a brisk pace over the bridge. As they crossed the border, Theodor's heart thrilled for joy. They were still in danger and would be for some time, but they had just experienced another miracle.

With the bridge behind them, Theodor and Ivan started planning their next step.

"Let's find somewhere to clean up a bit," Theodor suggested to Ivan. "If we look more civilized, we might appear less suspicious." Outside the city's perimeter, they spotted a farmhouse. As they usually had found farmers to be friendly, Ivan and Theodor walked up the quiet drive and knocked on the wooden door. No one answered.

---

* Psalm 50:15.

"They must be out in the fields," Theodor said.

"There's a well in the yard," Ivan pointed out. "Let's find a bucket and get some water. We still might be able to wash up somewhere." It had been two weeks since either of them had washed or shaved.

"Let's see if the barn is open," Theodor said.

"Good idea."

They drew some water from the well and carried it to the barn. With no one in sight, the two cautiously slid the barn door open a crack and slipped inside. Their eyes adjusted quickly, revealing stalls for horses and other animals. They took the bucket of water to a row of barrels lined up against one wall. Finding just the right spot, Ivan set the bucket on an overturned barrel while Theodor pulled out the razor that had been tucked in a pocket of his jacket. Theodor quickly shaved and then handed the razor to Ivan. As Theodor splashed his smooth cheeks with cold water, his attention snapped to the crunch of tires in the driveway in front of the house. "The owners are home," he whispered. "Let me check."

Theodor peeked out a crack in the door, then jumped back. Four Russian military policemen, with rifles over their shoulders, spilled out of a jeep. *Someone saw us after all,* Theodor realized. *Will they ever leave us alone?*

"Police," Theodor hissed to Ivan. "Don't move!" Ivan clenched the razor to his heart like a cross. Ivan looked at Theodor. Pray, his eyes implored. Theodor wasted no time. The two men froze against the wall. The curses and thumps of the searching police drew closer. One of them reached the barn door, sliding it wide open. A bright swath of light poured in. The officer, hunter eyes probing the recesses of the empty stalls, scanned the length of the now-illuminated barn. Once again, there was nowhere to hide.

Chapter 4

Theodor, although guided by wise and God-fearing parents, nevertheless grew up surrounded by the fanaticism and superstition that steeped his native Ukraine. Witches, ghosts, magicians, and spells existed beyond the shivers of campfire stories. Given power by ignorance, misguided beliefs, and authentic paranormal activity, it was a mind-set difficult to penetrate with the true gospel story.

At every busy intersection in his village, passersby crossed themselves as they passed large wooden crosses. There being no street lamps in the village, the crosses stood like gallows in the night. Even Theodor hated to pass by the local cemetery where six-foot-tall crosses at every grave cast their eerie shadows. It was hard for anyone to be untainted by this fear.

A beautiful apple tree, for example, within a black-painted courtyard had once lured neighborhood boys to steal its fruit. But then, loaded with apples, the young thieves could not get down from the tree, no matter how they struggled. In order to escape, it was reported, they had to leave the apples behind. "There's a spell on that tree," Theodor's classmates warned.

A local grocer, rumored to have magical powers, tantalized the children with his mysterious abilities. One day after school, Theodor witnessed these powers for himself. The man, after putting biscuits in a basket, stepped outside of his store. He asked the children to stand behind his back. As he threw the biscuits over his shoulders, the children quickly scooped them up, hiding the biscuits in various places. Somehow, the man knew exactly how many biscuits each child had snatched and where the biscuits were hidden.

Legend also surrounded a local hunchback, feared as a witch, who pastured her fat and healthy cows in the meadows on the other side of the nearby Prut River. "Keep your cows away from her, or she will cast a spell on them," the villagers warned. "She goes up to other people's cows and says, 'Oh, look at that pretty cow. She must give plenty of milk.' And from then on the cow stops giving milk and gets sick. The only choice the owners have left is to kill the cow for meat before it dies."

As for the Pawluks' cows, the locals considered them as Adventist as the Pawluks themselves, and were equally despised. "Keep your heretic cows away from our cows," the cowherders threatened, throwing stones at the Pawluks' bovines to keep them away from their own grazing herds.

Forced to move their cattle higher into the Carpathian Mountains to find pasture, Theodor once came across a bizarre little package lying on the ground. As he reached down to examine it, his little brother, Slawko, yelled at him.

"Don't touch it!"

Theodor jumped back. "Why not?"

"It was probably put there by a witch to cast a spell on someone."

"Oh," said Theodor, disgusted, picking it up. Examining the small bundle, Theodor found a few small slivers of wood, some human hair, several small bones, forest leaves, and some kind of animal skin as a wrapping.

"What if you get sick now?" Slawko worried.

"God will protect me," Theodor said. "I feel sorry for the person who believes in this type of witchcraft."

Near Theodor's home, the Prut River itself was a source of local legend. Without a bridge, the people forded the river on foot or by horse and wagon. In the rainy season as the river began to flood, crossings became treacherous. One particular section claimed many drowning victims. Villagers passing by that crossing in the night often heard ghostly voices calling for help.

One dark night Theodor walked toward home beside the Prut River. He had never believed the villagers' spooky tales himself, but as he neared the haunted crossing—a place with no houses or people—he grew uneasy. Suddenly, in front of him on the path appeared a nearly seven-foot-tall giant figure, holding up its right hand. In the darkness, Theodor mistook the form for that of his father coming to find him.

"Father?" he asked. "Here I am. Let's go home now."

The apparition remained silent.

A ghost! Theodor thought, terror seizing him. Too scared to bolt, he walked away, backtracking around the figure as fast as he could. Finally clear, Theodor broke into a run.

When Theodor arrived home, his face was as white as paper.

"What happened?" Onofre asked when he saw Theodor's pale face. Theodor relayed the riverbank encounter.

"Could it really have been a ghost of someone who had drowned?" Theodor asked.

Onofre shook his head. "It might have looked like one, but it wasn't."

"But what I saw was real, Father. It wasn't my imagination."

"I believe you," Onofre said. "But it wasn't a ghost. You know your Bible better than that. What does the Bible actually teach about death?"

"It teaches that the dead know nothing," Theodor said. "That death is like a dreamless sleep."

"Right."

"The priest teaches that the dead have immortal souls, and we either go to heaven or hell when we die," Theodor said.

"Yes. I was taught the same," said Onofre. "And there *are* some Bible texts that seem to support this, but it's a dangerous misunderstanding."

"What did I see, then? What are the ghosts and the voices that people talk about? There must be something behind all the stories."

"Of course there is. We know that fallen angels love to deceive people."

Theodor shuddered. "That doesn't make it less scary."

"Theo, as long as you serve the Lord, the evil one cannot touch you without God's permission," his father reassured. "God promises that 'he that dwelleth in the secret place of the most High shall abide under the shadow of the Almighty.'* You are safe with Him."

"I want to have faith like yours," Theodor told his father. There was nothing he wanted more.

—*—*—*

In the spring of 1938, Theodor, now thirteen, walked purposefully down the dirt road that led to the village plaza at the center of town. The Greek Orthodox church in which he had been christened stood majestically, its large domed roof glinting in the morning sun. Year after year, he walked this path with his classmates as they went to mandatory confession. The priest lived in a small rectory beside the church. The priest seemed fond of Theodor, despite Theodor's "heretical" father. Theodor had often visited the priest here and had even eaten meals with him, but now the thought of this visit made him queasy. For seven years the priest had taught Theodor the Greek Orthodox theology, and there was no easy way to tell the priest his decision.

"Good morning, Father," said Theodor, finding the priest in his office.

---

* Psalm 91:1.

"Why, Theodor," the priest said, smiling broadly. "What brings you here on such a fine day? Now that you've graduated from grade school, do you have so much free time that you can stop by to chat?" He lowered his eyebrows at Theodor. "Or, do we need to step into the confessional booth?"

"Well," said Theodor, swallowing, "I wanted to thank you for being such a good teacher to me all these years."

"Thank you, Theodor. Coming from you, I find that is quite the compliment."

"What do you mean, Father?"

"You know, Theodor. You never seemed very enthusiastic in religion class, though I must say you did earn a very good report card." Theodor shifted his feet. In spite of all the ridicule and punishment that he had to endure for not complying with his teachers in religious matters, he had earned good grades.

"Thank you, Father. I know you had a hard time with me sometimes, and I wanted to let you know that I think you did an excellent job teaching me."

"Well, Theodor, some young people take a while to accept all the teachings of the church, but I believe you're coming around."

"Father, I learned our theology well. That is one of the reasons why I had to come today." The priest looked at him quizzically. Theodor took a deep breath. "There is no easy way to say this, but I am asking for an official release to transfer my membership." There. He had said it.

The priest gazed at him, his eyes showing his concern. "Are you saying you wish to leave the church permanently? You must consider the gravity of what you are saying."

"Yes, Father. I have considered it very carefully, and I have decided to be baptized into the Seventh-day Adventist Church."

The priest groaned. "Theodor, you are still quite young to make such a major decision. Aren't you just thirteen?"

"Yes, but—"

"I know you are influenced by your father," the man interrupted.

"I know he means well, but he has been led astray. Now he wishes to lead you out of the fold, as well. You must be strong, Theodor, and resist this temptation. This is God's church, and any other teaching, especially the Seventh-day Adventist theology, is heresy. Do you know what this means?"

"I understand you, Father," said Theodor. "But I am making this decision based on my own studies. My father has influenced me, but I take everything he says and check it carefully in the Bible."

"Ah, Theodor," the priest said, nodding. "The Bible. You are too young to be attempting to read the Bible for yourself. My role as your shepherd is to help you interpret correctly what you read. I can see how you have been led astray without my guidance. I have not had the opportunity to answer all your questions."

"Yes, Father, I know what the Greek Orthodox Church teaches, but I need my questions answered from the Bible. You see, I have been comparing both the teachings of the Orthodox Church and the Seventh-day Adventist Church with the Bible."

"You are a good student, Theodor," said the priest. "You know that the Orthodox Church follows the Bible. God gave Saint Peter authority over the church, and the church leadership has held this position ever since."

"Yes, Father, I remember what the church teaches. However, I still have found that the teachings of this church are contrary to the Bible in many ways. The Seventh-day Adventist teachings, on the other hand, are more in harmony with the Bible."

"Theodor, are you trying to tell me that you have more knowledge of God and the Bible than I do?" The priest chuckled.

"No, Father," Theodor replied humbly, "but I feel it is very important to serve God according to His will and not to disobey Him."

"But it is not God's will that you leave this church, Theodor. You will be disobeying Him if you leave."

Theodor sighed and shook his head.

"Theodor, you are still a boy, and I am your spiritual father. I am not willing to let you leave. You would regret this deeply some-day."

I can't join any other church unless I have his written permission. Theodor suppressed his panic with a silent prayer. "Father, I was baptized as an infant in this church thirteen years ago, and I have been counted as a member ever since, but my heart and mind are not here. Without disrespect to you, Father, I now wish no part of it. My conscience does not allow it."

Despite Theodor's persistence, the priest held his ground. "Theodor, I will be glad to study with you more and show you the right path. I have confidence that you will reconsider when you understand where you have been led astray." He smiled.

"Thank you, Father," said Theodor. "But I won't be changing my mind." The priest devoted more than an hour trying to convince Theodor to remain a member of his church, but to no avail. At long last, the priest scribbled out the release form on paper, made a note to himself to change the records in the books, and handed Theodor his longed-for signature.

"I'm very sorry to see you go," the priest said. "It grieves both me and God to see you choose against Him. I have done what I can for you, but I see that you are determined."

"Thank you, Father," Theodor said, a huge weight sliding off him. "You have been kind to me, in spite of everything. Thank you."

The priest waved his hand goodbye while his lips curved into a small, sad smile.

Clutching the release form, Theodor tried to walk calmly from the room. Sorry to disappoint the priest but relieved beyond words, Theodor felt excitement coursing through him. Now he was free to join any church he wished.

Theodor went straight to the Seventh-day Adventist church. The small church in Kolomeya did not have a baptistry, but one of the church members had property bordering the Prut River. Theodor and the pastor, Stefan Smyk, made plans to hold the baptism there. They set a Sunday date for his baptism to accommodate nonchurch members who might wish to attend. Theodor told everyone he knew about the upcoming event. The word spread rapidly.

Baptism by immersion is a symbol of the death, burial, and resurrection of Jesus. In this public declaration of commitment to Christ, Theodor would show that he, too, was willing to die to his own interests and to live his life always for God. But baptism also meant incurring the scorn and persecution of many in the community.

The little church gathered at the home by the river that Sunday to hear the baptismal sermon. Following the sermon the plan was to go with Theodor to the river. It was a solemn, yet joyful occasion for all. During the sermon, however, the members began to hear the restless noise of a crowd gathering by the riverbank.

Are that many people interested in my baptism? Theodor wondered, trying to concentrate on the sermon. Suddenly the door of the home opened and two armed policemen from the nearby city of Kolomeya walked into the meeting.

"Can we help you?" asked Pastor Smyk from the front. The congregation turned toward the door as the policemen stood in the entrance.

"We heard there's going to be a baptism at the river today," one officer said.

"Yes." The preacher nodded.

"We don't think that's such a good idea," laughed the other.

"Oh?"

"There are almost a thousand people outside on the riverbank waiting to see the baptism, and they don't look friendly."

"What do you mean?" asked Pastor Smyk.

"They're all armed, nearly every one of them," the officer explained. "Knives, clubs, sticks." A quiet murmur rippled through the worshipers. "We asked what all the commotion was about and were told they were getting ready to stop a baptism. I doubt you'd make it out of that river alive."

Theodor shivered.

"What if we have your protection?" Pastor Smyk asked.

One officer snorted. The other laughed. "Two policemen are simply no match for that many hostile people."

"What do you suggest?" the pastor continued.

"Postpone your baptism for now and, without any announcement, have the baptism in some other area at some other time."

Pastor Smyk nodded. "Thank you. Will you spread the word that there will not be a baptism today after all?"

The policemen nodded and were gone.

The congregation sat together for a moment in silence. Theodor felt crushed. The pastor turned to where the Pawluk family sat.

"This is a great disappointment for the whole church, Theodor. I know that it is for you." The congregation murmured sympathetically. "There is nothing we can do," the pastor continued. Theodor nodded. His mother squeezed his shoulder. "Those people by the riverbank have never witnessed a baptism by immersion, only by sprinkling," the pastor added. "I suppose they think they are helping God by coming out to attack us 'heretics.' I'm sorry, but we must reschedule your baptism for another time."

Theodor heard distant voices outside. "There will be no baptism today. Go on home."

A general uproar followed. "We've been waiting for hours. What do you mean?"

"There will be no baptism at this time," the policemen repeated. "It's time to leave."

"All this waiting for nothing?" The crowd grumbled in disappointment.

"Let me finish my sermon," Pastor Smyk addressed his congregation. "Then we'll make new plans. I think it wise to remain here until the crowd is gone."

Everyone agreed. After the sermon, they began making new plans for Theodor's baptism. "We need another place where there is enough water," someone said.

"Let's have it high up in the Carpathian Mountains near Huculivka," Theodor's father suggested. "There's a small Seventh-day Adventist church there, and I know of a beautiful little stream flowing between the mountains."

"A stream isn't deep enough for immersion, is it?" someone asked.

"We'll dig a small pool by the stream. That should do it," Theodor's father replied.

"There may be others who would like to be baptized then too," the pastor added. "With two churches attending, it will be a special time."

"Let's not publicize *this* baptism," someone said, laughing nervously. Everyone agreed. After the riverbank crowd dispersed, the church members quietly slipped out, heading home.

Later during that summer of 1938, Theodor and several other candidates were baptized in a cold mountain pool. The two participating churches officially welcomed them into the church family. Pastor Andrew Maszczak, editor of *Znaky Chasy,* the Ukrainian version of *Signs of the Times,* officiated. This time there was no trouble. Stepping out of the pool, dripping with both water and joy, Theodor embraced his father and mother. Onofre presented him with a Bible of his own. It was a small edition, only about four by five inches, but to Theodor it was the prize of his life. Little could he know how much this little Bible would come to mean in the years ahead.

------*---*

"Theo," his father said, working with his son at the weaver's bench one day soon after the baptism. "You have graduated from school, and you've chosen to follow God. It's time for you to make another decision." Onofre's fingers deftly wove the colorful thread back and forth across the loom.

"But, Father," Theodor said, grinning. "I think I'm really too young to get married just yet."

"Eh?" His father's eyebrows shot up. "You know I didn't mean *that,* you rascal, but you really do need to choose a profession."

Theodor sighed. "I know, Father. I've been thinking about it, too, but I just don't know what to do."

"What are you considering?"

"Well, most of my friends are going to work in their family businesses or farms, but . . ." Theodor paused.

"You don't want to be a weaver, do you?" his father said, smiling. "Is there another trade that you'd like to learn?"

"I've considered several of them. Many of my classmates are getting apprenticeships with local craftsmen—shoemakers, blacksmiths, builders, bakers. But there's really only one thing I want to do."

"What's that?" his father asked.

"I want to serve the Lord." Theodor glanced at the folded piles of his father's carefully woven fabric. "I know I can serve the Lord in any profession or trade, like you have all your life, doing everything to the glory of God. I've listened to you share your faith with your customers, and I've gone with you every Sabbath to one of the four churches you started."

"So you want to go into the ministry?"

"Yes."

His father put down his work and turned to Theodor. A smile spread across his face.

"Can you see me as a pastor?" Theodor asked.

Onofre laughed. "It is a hard profession, but you are strong and dedicated. If that's what you feel God calling you to do, then I know you can do it. I think we should talk to Pastor Smyk."

After talking about it at home and with their pastor, they concluded, unanimously, that Theodor should pursue additional education preparing for the ministry. That education would be far away from Kornich, because their denomination had no schools in the vicinity.

"The Seventh-day Adventist denomination has a custom that anyone who wants to enter the ministry should have at least three years of colporteuring experience first, before going to school," Pastor Smyk explained. It was a common practice at that time throughout Europe. "Selling Adventist Christian literature door to door will help you develop many qualities necessary for being a pastor—faith, reliance on God, self-confidence, people skills, persuasive skills, and leadership skills, to name a few."

"That makes sense," Theodor said. "I've already been working part time as a colporteur during the summers. Now I'll just become one full time. Do I have to go by myself?"

"Oh, no. Meroslaw Sapowich, one of our members at the Huculivka church, has also chosen to work as a colporteur. He is sixteen, only two years older than you are, and will be a fine person to team with."

Theodor liked Meroslaw. Sincere and honest, Meroslaw taught Theodor what to say at each door. Together they traveled the countryside, selling Christian books. Once Theodor learned the ropes, Meroslaw worked one side of the street while Theodor canvassed the other. When the workweek was completed, the two looked for a church to attend on Sabbath.

In the 1930s, the colporteuring business was very successful. There were no televisions to watch, and very few villagers owned radios. Only the larger cities offered newspapers, and even then, not many people subscribed to them. Thus, after the farmers were finished working the fields, they had time to read, especially during the winter.

The one difficulty the young colporteurs faced in the Ukraine was that the farmers already had nearly everything they needed for living, except money. In order to make a sale, Theodor and Meroslaw had to accept the farmers' produce as payment for their books. Accordingly, Theodor and his friend always carried a couple bags on their shoulders. Closed at each end, the bags opened in the middle. Into these bags they put the grain and beans that the farmers gave in exchange for literature.

When the bags got too heavy, the colporteurs sold their produce to the village storehouse. The price received gave some idea of what to charge for their books. In some ways, carrying grain and beans was better than carrying cash. Once, early on, when Theodor was colporteuring alone, the police detained him and confiscated all his books and money. But who wants to be bothered with grain?

Theodor and Meroslaw traveled on foot, working each village for a few days until they had canvassed the whole town. When they ran out of literature, their supplier sent more books to designated post offices. With no motels to stay in, Theodor and Meroslaw often lodged with local farmers, offering their books in lieu of payment for a place to sleep. This also provided an opportunity to share with their hosts about their faith and the good news of God's saving grace. Many times, Theodor and Meroslaw wished they could stay with the farmers a while longer, but duty urged them to keep moving on.

Fridays they worked only until lunchtime, preparing for the Sabbath in the afternoon. In the Ukraine, people had a bath only once a week. The young men had theirs on Friday, taking an afternoon excursion to the village public baths.

Sabbaths were always special. Theodor and Meroslaw looked for a Seventh-day Adventist church to attend and often were requested to share their testimonies and colporteuring experiences with the congregation. After church, some family would invariably invite the two hungry young men home for lunch.

Theodor never looked forward to plying their wares in the cities as it was significantly more dangerous than in the villages. Though the laws of the state guaranteed religious freedom, those laws were seldom enforced. In Poland, the governing power lay in the hands of the local priests. If one found out that Theodor and Meroslaw were selling Christian books from another denomination in that priest's area, he often sent the police after the young salesmen. Confiscating their books and their proceeds, the police made it clear that Theodor and Meroslaw were not welcome. In the villages, however, they remained free from police harassment.

As a rule, Theodor and Meroslaw made an effort to visit every house in a village; poor or rich, it did not matter. One time, though, with sales flowing briskly in a particularly large village, Theodor and Meroslaw decided to call it quits early. They had sold lots of books and started heading out of town.

"Hey there. What are you doing?" a shout came from the hill above them.

"Uh-oh," whispered Meroslaw. "I think we overlooked a few houses on the top of the hill."

"Pretend you didn't hear them." Theodor and his friend picked up their pace.

"You're not going anywhere!" another voice shouted. "Stop them."

"Great!" Meroslaw groaned. A wave of fear hit Theodor.

"They're starting to chase us, and they don't seem very friendly," Theodor said, the pitch of his voice rising. The shouts grew nearer. Theodor and Meroslaw said a silent prayer and had no choice but to stop and wait for the approaching crowd.

The villagers caught up to them, and a gruff man stepped forward.

"What were you doing all day in our village?" the man demanded.

"We were selling Christian literature." Meroslaw answered.

"Do you have permission from the authorities to do that?" another man asked.

"No," replied Theodor, trying to look as if he didn't care.

"Why did you pass us by and not give us the courtesy of seeing your books?" the first man asked. "Maybe we would have bought some, but you totally ignored us."

"Well, we, uh . . ." Theodor and Meroslaw looked chagrined. They were embarrassed and ashamed of their negligence.

"Show us all your books," demanded another villager, pointing at the heavy sacks.

Theodor and Meroslaw set down their bags and unzipped them, watching in amazement as the villagers debated which books to buy.

Theodor and Meroslaw sold many books at the impromptu gathering. The sun was melting into the western fields as the villagers climbed back up the hill to their homes. Theodor and Meroslaw slung much lighter sacks on their backs and trudged on.

"Well, what do you know? That was the best sale of the day," Theodor said, exhilarated, still trying to process what had just happened.

"Next time we're thinking of quitting early, we'll have to remember this," Meroslaw exclaimed, thumping his friend on the back.

"When I become a pastor, I'll think twice about overlooking that last house to visit or ignoring the unlikely convert," Theodor agreed.

"People look on the outside," Meroslaw said, paraphrasing a Bible passage, "but God knows the heart."

Theodor nodded. As they neared that night's lodging, Theodor and Meroslaw speculated about all God might have in store for them when they became ministers. Nothing felt impossible after the experiences the two had faced colporteuring. That evening, the future glowed bright with promise.

Unfortunately, within a year, the wheels flew off of Theodor's plans, landing him stuck, along with the rest of Europe, in an unforeseen bog. On September 1, 1939, Hitler attacked Poland from the west. On September 17, 1939, Stalin attacked Poland from the east, his sights on the Ukraine, and soon invaded the entire West Ukraine territory. In Theodor's area there was no resistance. The Soviets took over everything, including his dreams.

Chapter 5

"Are there any questions?" the *politruk,* a Russian "political instructor," purred, closing his weekly lecture. His words echoed off the bare walls of the school auditorium, where Onofre and four hundred other villagers sat. Theodor's father raised his hand. The instructor, a short man with graying hair, turned warmly toward Onofre. "Yes, Onofre," he said. While his tone seemed affable, Onofre felt subtle claws retracting and expanding over the students, who seemed more like mice trapped in a corner.

"I am a Seventh-day Adventist. Many here are Greek Orthodox Christians. Will we be allowed to take off Saturday or Sunday from work, according to our convictions, for religious reasons?" Onofre asked. The villagers were incredulous at his audacity.

"Ah, your Saturday Sabbath, right?" the teacher said, nodding, as if he knew all about it. "I can see how this might concern you." Onofre said nothing. He clasped his hands together in his lap. He had learned well the art of keeping quiet, reading the gestures and body language of those around him, and being alert. All he wanted right now was to be anonymous, to blend in with the other students compliant in their seats, but he had to know the answer.

The politruk chuckled. He tapped his fingers together pointedly. *Sharpening,* Onofre thought.

"Do you expect to have your Sabbaths off on a first-class job where hundreds of people are working, where your job is connected to everyone else's job?" the man continued. "Do you think you can put your tools down in a factory for a day and expect everybody to wait for you to come back?" He laughed, shaking his head. "No. If you expect special treatment, you'll have to try to find some type of job where no one must depend on you." Onofre nodded his head in understanding and leaned back in his chair. The instructor smiled benevolently. "Good luck with that."

Onofre shifted in his seat. Though nods of agreement and approval peppered the class, he sensed the forced camaraderie and thinly veiled tension. Despite the age gap and his instructor's strange, stilted vocabulary, Onofre could easily imagine himself sitting in Theodor's religion class, awkward and out of place. But now, instead of Greek Orthodox teaching, it was the catechism of Communism—atheism, obedience, and "elusive" equality.

"And while we are on the subject of religion," the politruk emphasized each word, "you must understand that the Soviet Union's government is atheistic. Any kind of religious activity is discouraged." The man walked down the narrow aisle between rows.

No more colporteuring for Theodor, Onofre thought sadly. It had been several weeks now since the Soviets had occupied the entire region, but Theodor had still held on to hope that life would return to normal.

"Religion is an opiate and an exploitation of the working-class people, money, and time." The teacher pounded his fists together. A few murmurs of consent broke the silence in the class. "Therefore," the politruk stressed, "all religious proselytizing or open discussion of religious subjects is illegal in the Soviet Union. There will be no printing or selling of religious literature."

The villagers sitting in the rough chairs in rows around him waited out the lecture, dutifully listening to the politruk explain the ins and outs, the rights and wrongs of being a good citizen in the Soviet system. With its takeover, the Soviet officers had promptly divided the villages into small precincts. In each of these little districts, the government required attendance at this indoctrination class from at least one person of each household once a week. Because the Russian and Ukrainian languages were similar, all the villagers understood their conqueror's language and meaning well enough. With a little time, all too well.

Highly interested in the citizens' private lives and, it seemed, their well-being, the politruk remembered everyone's names, as well as their individual problems. Over the six-month education, many of the villagers opened up with their interested instructor, telling him all about their lives. The politruk learned who had money, who had higher education, who asked questions. Onofre tried to keep his mouth closed and to be inconspicuous.

Shortly after the politruk left the area and the weekly classes ended, strange events unsettled the community. Houses mysteriously emptied. Wagons full of furniture were pulled down the road. Entire families disappeared overnight. No one spoke of it. A nameless horror hovered over each household, invading their peace and robbing them of their ease, their safety, and their joy. In hushed conversations around the dinner table, Onofre, who served as head elder of his church, Caroline, and their pastor, Stefan Smyk, discussed with each other what these events might mean for their families and the church. Theodor was old enough to participate in the sober conversation.

"It's only a matter of time until it happens to us," Onofre confided. "Last night another neighbor's family disappeared."

"Where did they go?" Caroline asked.

"Just gone," Onofre replied. "More families are disappearing every day—or night, rather—mostly the wealthy and the intellectuals. Some of my clients have never returned to pick up their weaving orders."

"You mean someone just comes and takes away the family in the middle of the night?" Caroline asked in shock. "With their children?"

"Yes," Pastor Smyk confirmed. "Families are here one day, and the next their house is silent, soon emptied of all their furniture and belongings."

"How could anyone do that?" Theodor questioned, slapping the table. "Who could be so barbaric?" He, too, had seen wagons of furniture being hauled down the roads. He had just supposed a family was moving. But lately, he saw more of these wagons than usual. Then he remembered the politruk's seemingly innocent interest in everybody's lives. The honeymoon was over.

"The KGB," his father answered. "At least, that's the rumor."

"Who?" asked Caroline.

"The Committee for State Security. Their job is to watch for any danger threatening the government."

"But how are these families a threat to the government?"

"Apparently, the rich and educated people are always a threat to the Soviets."

"It doesn't take much for one to be arrested, I've discovered," said Pastor Smyk. "Any suspicious characters are already guilty as far as the KGB is concerned."

"But who reports them?" Caroline prodded.

"There are always sympathizers," Onofre admitted, "who are glad to betray the rest. Many of these people are poor and uneducated and accustomed to government handouts—the Soviet Union promotes equality, right? All someone has to do is complain to the Soviet officials that they have worked for some of these affluent people in the past and haven't been paid well." Theodor scoured his memory for a reason they would come for his own family, playing absentmindedly with his empty cup.

"Don't these people get a chance to speak up and demonstrate their support for the government?" Caroline asked.

"They don't get a fair hearing. There's no judge, no jury, no rights—the KGB does it all at night when there's no one to observe," Onofre said.

"But where do they take them?" Caroline insisted.

"Siberia," Onofre answered. Theodor shuddered.

"Where is Siberia?" Theodor's younger sister, Daria, whispered to her brothers.

"Far away. Up north," Slawko whispered back.

"It's a frozen wasteland up there," Theodor added. "All I know is that there are prison camps there where they make people work until they die."

"Even little kids?" asked Daria, her face turning pale.

"I think they send the kids to an orphanage," Slawko said. That didn't make Daria feel any better.

"Shhh," their mother hissed. "Boys, don't scare your sister."

"Siberia," repeated Onofre to Pastor Smyk. This one little word would prove an invisible noose around everyone's neck. Soon, hardly a family in the entire Soviet Union would turn in for the night with the assurance that they would wake up in the morning in their own beds.

"Disobedience, wealth, intelligence, education, or simply suspicious behavior can mean arrest and captivity, never to return," added the pastor. "And . . ." he paused and put his head in his hands.

"Worship?" Caroline asked.

"*Especially* worship," said the pastor, lifting his face. "Look, the fact is that I'm afraid about the safety of our church members. We must be extremely cautious. I think it's in our church members' best interest that we stop meeting together on Sabbath, at least for a while."

Onofre nodded his head in agreement.

"But we can't stop worshiping on Sabbath!" Caroline exclaimed.

"Oh no," said Onofre. "We will still keep the Sabbath, but on our own with our families for now. It's just too dangerous. I know we are being watched, but just how closely I don't know."

"But what about your job, Pastor?" Caroline asked.

Pastor Smyk sighed. "I think it best that I quit as your official pastor for now and that I go to work in some other trade." The family around the table winced.

Has it come to this? thought Theodor.

"What will you do?" asked Onofre. His tone of voice revealed his concern.

"I used to make shoes with my father," said Pastor Smyk. "I plan to work as a cobbler in Kolomeya. There is always a need for this service. What about yourself, Onofre? How's your business doing under the new government?"

"I'm staying on our farm here and carrying on my weaving business as before," Onofre said. "I am aware that the Soviets do not approve of free enterprise—"

"Don't you mean 'tyranny and exploitation of the working class'?" interrupted Theodor sarcastically.

"You learned your lessons well," Onofre respond wryly. "But I think because I do not employ other people and simply work by myself, they don't seem to care. At least they haven't said anything to me about it yet."

"What about you, Theodor?" asked Pastor Smyk. "I know you are devastated about giving up your plans for the ministry."

Theodor nodded, tracing his finger on the rough grain of the wooden table. He didn't answer right away.

"This Soviet occupation may not last forever, so don't give up hope," the pastor comforted. "In the meantime, are you going to join the Komsomol Party for young Soviet citizens? You will have to join when you are twenty, but now, if you're not involved, your entire family may be in danger."

Theodor gulped. He didn't want to be responsible for his family's deportation, but he knew the kinds of things that happened in this state-sponsored, atheistic club. "I know," he said. "But the last thing I will be is responsible for sending people to Siberia. They want members to discuss who may be a danger to the government."

"A gossip session," said Caroline.

"Sort of," said Theodor. "If I join the collective farm down the road, I can be exempt for a while. I just want to mind my own business."

"What's a collective farm?" piped up Daria.

"All the farm workers share the labor, and then the crops will be divided between us. We'll get paid with the produce from the farm.

Any money earned will be divided equally—all the same amount, they tell us.* Sounds good, but I'm worried."

"Why?" Caroline asked.

"I'm sure they won't let me take the Sabbath off," Theodor said. "You remember the politruk's statements?"

Onofre nodded.

"God will provide a way," Pastor Smyk reassured. "He won't let you down."

Theodor thought of all the disappointments he had already faced in his young life. *How can the pastor-turned-shoemaker be so optimistic?*

Theodor managed a small smile "I hope you're right, Pastor."

Throughout the Soviet occupation, Theodor and his family tried to live quiet, inconspicuous lives, showing respect and cooperation for the Soviet government at every opportunity. On every Soviet national holiday, the family displayed portraits of Stalin and Molotov, the Soviet foreign minister, on their front gate, just as the other neighbors did, for all to see.

Theodor found most of his jobs on the collective farm varied and interesting. He knew how to work hard, and he challenged himself by trying to accomplish each job as quickly as possible. Theodor especially enjoyed working in the field all by himself; there was no one to bother him with the omnipresent questions about how he and his family liked the new Soviet system.

Once, when assigned to plow a field with two young horses, Theodor finished the job far more quickly than expected. The next day his supervisors sent him to the same place to smooth the ground with a harrow in preparation for sowing the seeds. Partly because his horses had so much energy, Theodor again worked quickly and completed harrowing the field in record time.

---

* Theodor would soon realize that in this "working-class paradise," the state took its part first—between 50 and 70 percent—and then the working class received the leftovers.

A few days later an article appeared in the local newspaper. "Theodor Pawluk breaks the speed record in harrowing a field." Theodor glowed with pride to know his hard work had been noticed—that is, until he returned to work the next day.

"Now we're expected to do the same amount of work," his fellow workers grumbled. "Watch out, or you're going to make the rest of us look bad." Theodor understood the implied threat.

The farm officials made Theodor, their youngest worker, their chauffeur—not with a car, because they did not have one—but with a horse and wagon. Several times a week the farm officials attended business meetings in the city, with Theodor at the reins.

Other times the officials sent Theodor to the city bazaar in Kolomeya to sell vegetables grown on the collective farm—carrots, cabbages, onions, cauliflowers, radishes, cucumbers, garlic cloves, and tomatoes. As he headed out with the wagon full of fresh produce, Theodor recognized the responsibility he'd been given. Selling those vegetables was one of the few sources of income for the farm.

Despite his initial worry, Theodor had no difficulty in getting Sabbaths off. The managers on the farm were the people from his own village. "The sun is shining on the bottom of the window board," the older farm officials would tell him Friday afternoon, with a knowing wink. "Go home now. Your father is waiting for you."

His peers, the younger officials in the village were not as nice.

One cold winter Saturday, Onofre took Theodor on a Sabbath visit to the home of an older widow and her two daughters.

Taking pains to be inconspicuous, they followed lonely paths between snow-covered fields, far from prying eyes. After studying the Bible lesson with the family and closing the short visit with prayer, Theodor and his father retraced their path home, trusting that no one had seen them traveling on their Sabbath day.

That Sunday evening, Theodor decided to attend a gathering of the village young people at the recreation hall. He knew nearly everyone from school and did not want to appear too different or uninvolved, particularly since he had not joined the youth Komsomol Party.

At the entrance, one young member of the Communist Party blocked his way.

"You can't come in," he announced, his voice intentionally loud. The social chatter in the hall quieted as heads turned to stare at Theodor.

"Why not?" Theodor asked.

"Because you were at the Aschenbrenners' house on Saturday. You studied the Bible with them."

At the word *Bible,* all conversation in the hall ceased.

Theodor swallowed, not knowing how to respond.

The youth smirked. "You cannot join in both activities. If you wish, go back to the Aschenbrenners."

Theodor turned away, the door slamming behind him. Now he knew just how closely he and his family were being watched.

One day when Theodor reported for work, the foreman handed him and another worker a paper with a local address. "You are to go to this house and pick up all the furniture and appliances that you find there," the foreman directed. "Load it all and bring everything back to the farm." Theodor nodded, trying not to show emotion. He suspected the worst.

"Remember one thing," the foreman warned the young men. "Do not talk with anyone about this, not even with each other. Do not ask questions, and do not give answers. Do you understand?"

"Yes, sir," Theodor replied, avoiding eye contact. He gripped the paper in his hand and started for the door.

"Theodor," the foreman called. "Do not talk to the neighbors either."

"Yes, sir."

The morning sun warmed Theodor's back. A fresh breeze ruffled his hair. Theodor did not notice, though, as he and his helper hitched the horses to a large wagon. Theodor usually loved to be on the road, listening to the rattle of the wagon and the *clip-clop* cadence of the horses. This day was different; he would rather be doing almost anything else.

Passing neighbor farmers working in their fields, children playing in farmyards, and women hanging laundry on clotheslines, Theodor neared the fated farm. He imagined cold stares and an icy chill descending over the neighborhood as he turned in at the farmyard gate, parking the wagon near the front door.

A hungry cat meowed on the front steps. A dog wandered around the deserted farmyard, scavenging for food. Theodor pictured with painful clarity what must have happened at this home during the predawn hours. He longed to disappear, but the large wagon and the two horses attracted attention.

The KGB.

Inside the house, a half-eaten meal lay spread out on the table, gathering flies. Children's toys lay scattered on the floor, and homemade dolls were abandoned in empty beds. After Theodor and his helper cleared the dishes from the table, Theodor threw the scraps outside for the eager cat and dog. Hoisting the table, the two workers hauled it out to the wagon, bringing out the chairs next. Chagrined, Theodor noticed a small group of neighbors entering the farmyard gate. He turned away quickly, loading more furniture.

"Where are you taking all this?" one farmer asked when Theodor reemerged, the gruff voice breaking the dreadful silence. Theodor started to speak, but then, remembering the foreman's orders, pressed his lips together. His helper shook his head.

"Why won't you at least talk with us?" one neighbor woman pleaded. "These were good people, a wonderful family. Why were they taken away?" Theodor stalked back into the house, his heart breaking.

"It's not fair," another woman cried but was hushed by another. "Who will listen to us? Our neighbors were here yesterday—but now they're gone. Gone!" Theodor wanted to explain that he had no idea why the family had been taken away and that he didn't want to be involved either, but fear restrained him. He glanced at his helper, knowing that one peep out of his mouth could mean the deportation of his own entire family.

"Shhhh," he heard another voice caution, "These fellows are in cahoots with the KGB. They might come for us next."

"Why won't they leave us alone?"

Theodor and his partner finished the onerous task in silence. The thought of the KGB and their nighttime raids filled him with horror. And now he was a part of it. Many times during the following months, Theodor was asked to remove furniture from other vacated houses.

——————*———*

One clear summer day on the streets of Kolomeya, while his horses switched their tails at flies, Theodor lounged in the back of his wagon waiting for the collective farm officials to return from their meeting. The attack came out of nowhere. Suddenly, the whole city erupted in confusion. Theodor sat bolt upright, staring at gray German bombers flying low over the city, their roar deafening. Explosions blasted flames and debris high into the air. People ran screaming, looking for places to hide. Staccato machine gun blasts combined with the whistle of falling bombs terrified the horses, who neighed and lunged in terror. Theodor tried to calm the animals. Not wanting to abandon them, he sat wide-eyed and cringing in the wagon as a bomb splintered an apartment complex on his right. Then another bomb exploded on his left.

As the bombs continued to pound Kolomeya on June 22, 1941, Theodor couldn't know that the Communist system—after one year, eight months, and twenty-five days—had come to its end in his area.

He had fainted in his seat.

Chapter 6

When Theodor awoke, he found himself flat on his back in a damp and dank-smelling cellar. Bewildered, he noted in the darkness around him the indistinct silhouettes of people crouching. Explosions still shook the ground as the muffled drone of airplanes filtered into the darkness. In the distance a siren wailed.

"What's happening?" he asked, rubbing his head.

"The Germans just attacked us," someone said, reminding him.

"Where am I?"

"In a basement. We saw you slumped over a wagon seat, unconscious, and we pulled you down here with us. Planes are flying so low that their soldiers are firing machine guns down the streets as they go by. You are lucky to be alive!"

Theodor sat up, hugging his knees. *I hope the horses are OK,* he thought. An absurd idea nearly made him chuckle. *I don't think I'll have to go back to work today.*

The attack lasted only a few minutes longer, but when the people emerged from the basement into the bright sunlight, they found a different city from the one they had known less than an hour before. The horses were gone. *Good,* Theodor thought, *that means that they're still alive.* People were standing around in shock, surveying the wreckage. Some were calling, looking for loved ones. Others were moaning or crying. Theodor noticed a streak of military green running through the debris. A Russian soldier. Then he saw another and another. They were headed out of town for the air force base.

"The Russians are all leaving," someone exclaimed, pointing toward the retreating military personnel. "They're afraid of the Germans."

Can it be true? Theodor hardly dared to hope. On his way home to check on his family, Theodor saw more fleeing Russians. *We're delivered.* The delightful thought surged like his adrenaline. Passing the collective farm, he saw that the fields and gardens, usually filled with laborers, were empty.

Onofre and Caroline rejoiced to see him home safely, especially after hearing his tale.

"No bombing out here in the country," his father reported, "but knowing how often you are in the city on business, we're glad to see that you are safe."

Learning that the Russian army had indeed packed up all their military hardware and were leaving the area, Theodor and a few other boys sneaked out to the Russian military airport only two kilometers away. "Let's see if they left anything behind," a friend suggested. But on arriving, the boys discovered to their horror that some of the Russian soldiers were still there.

"Get out of here, varmints," they roared. One of the soldiers grabbed his machine gun and opened fire on the boys. The rest of the soldiers followed suit. Bullets whizzed by Theodor and his companions.

"Run!" he shouted, as the boys ducked and scrambled for shelter. Chastened but unharmed, the young men crept back home.

Although Theodor had often dreamed of the day when Communism would end in his country, his relief was short-lived. For the three days that it took the German army to arrive, the country had no government. Theodor thought he had been scared before, but now, without security, protection, or law enforcement in the surrounding areas, these days were the most frightening of his life.

Anarchy reigned as angry and evil men, restraints thrown off, mistreated, beat, and killed those who had once cooperated with the Soviets. Those who had joined the Communist Party and the Komsomol Party for youth, all who had participated in the hated regime's program were subjects of special wrath. Villains stuffed chimneys while families were still inside their homes, suffocating everyone. Some burned homes and barns, while others looted, stole, and murdered. No one was safe during the days of lawlessness. Theodor and his family cowered in their home, pleading for divine protection.

A passage from Theodor's small Bible reminded him to never take for granted a life of peace. Let "supplication, prayers, intercessions, and giving of thanks be made for all men; For kings, and for all that are in authority; that we may lead a quiet and peaceable life in all godliness and honesty."* How Theodor longed for the quiet days he had known as a child. Even though he and his family had endured many hardships for their faith, they had never before experienced such sustained fear and uncertainty. As much as they dreaded the new regime, they looked forward to the stability this latest government would bring.

When the German army finally occupied the Ukraine, the victors restored social order to the area. To the surprise and relief of the Ukrainian people, they were allowed to form their own local governments and police forces. The Germans weren't interested in the Ukrainians' everyday lives or religion, so believers were free to worship openly again. At least in the rural areas.

But in the cities where church members had to work in the defense factories for the government, they could not take the Sabbath off because the workweek extended until noon every Saturday. Church life now mostly restored, Pastor Smyk returned from shoemaking to the pulpits of his four little churches, and the Pawluk family began attending church once more. During wartime the believers had little church literature, but they still had their Bibles.

---

* 1 Timothy 2:1, 2.

The German government's first priority lay in uniting the whole of Europe. A "clean" society was Germany's goal, and, after defeating Communism in the Ukraine, the Nazis lost no time in starting the "cleansing." First, they rounded up all the Gypsies and took them away. No one knew where. Then the homeless and beggars disappeared off the streets. Convicted or suspected child molesters and homosexuals also disappeared. The government swept up all criminals and threw them behind bars—or worse. For ten days in the central plaza of Kolomeya, for example, in view of all, the Nazis hung a sex offender from a pillar, an inscription below detailing his crime.

Though Theodor, his family, and many of their Protestant countrymen had experienced mistreatment for their faith, Theodor was not prepared for the brutality the new regime practiced against the Jews. He was even less prepared to witness the anti-Semitism and virulent cruelty of his fellow Ukrainians.

One day Theodor stared at the grotesque caricature of a Jewish man on the cover of a magazine. The man looked disfigured and unattractive. *"Schmeizt sie raus die Juden bande aus unseren Vaterlande,"* the headline shouted in bold black letters. "Throw the Jewish gang out of our Fatherland." Later that week, a huge billboard appeared in a prominent place with the same message and illustrated with similar depictions of the deformed Jewish people. *What?* thought Theodor, outraged. *Aren't the Jews part of our society too? What's going on?*

"They're now attacking innocent Jews who aren't a threat to the German people," Theodor complained to his father, who had also been disturbed by the new billboards. "No one seems to mind. I don't understand."

Onofre, who worked steadily at his loom, nodded sadly. "It's not really a surprise, is it?" his father asked. "The Greek Orthodox Church has pounded home the point in their services and in the schools that Jesus was crucified by the Jews."

"I remember," Theodor said, thinking of his recent school days. "Since the time I started school, the priest would describe all that

Jesus suffered and then accuse the Jews alone of being responsible. My classmates hated the Jews." He shuddered, recalling their venom.

"The people's distaste against the Jewish race runs very high," his father agreed. "The Orthodox Church has taught the people that they were doing God a favor by punishing the Jews for their sins."

"But we believe that it was all of our sins that sent Him to the cross," Theodor reflected. "The Jews are no more guilty of killing Him by their sins than we are by our own." Again his father nodded.

"But they have never learned this," Onofre said, sighing. He stopped his weaving to tie on more thread. "The people around us have always persecuted the Jews, which helps explain their dislike for us, because we also keep what they call the 'Jewish Sabbath.' "

"Before the Germans came," Theodor said, "Jewish salesmen would sometimes ride from village to village with their horse and wagons, buying young calves from the farmers for meat in the city."

"Yes," his father said. "We sold to them ourselves."

"Whenever they passed near where my classmates were pasturing their cattle, the boys would hurl stones from the highway at them and their calves," Theodor continued. "Sometimes the men barely escaped with their lives, and no one would try to stop it."

"I remember you telling me about it," said Onofre. "In fact, adults afterward joked about it and bragged about their children."

Theodor groaned. "Now the Nazis have given people permission to express their hostilities openly. Some of the people from the city seem just as savage as the Nazis, sometimes more so."

With the odious slogans receiving enthusiastic support, the Nazis were bold in their persecution of the Jews in the newly occupied territory. In Germany, many citizens did not know about Dachau, Auschwitz, Theresianstadt, and other concentration camps. Their newspapers reported no exterminations, nor did German radio mention the atrocities happening within their borders. But in the Ukraine and neighboring territories, no concentration camps were needed to conceal the Nazi's cruelty against the Jews. The cruelty was welcomed.*

The persecution of the Jews had reached a turning point on November 10, 1938. A few days earlier in Paris, a young Jew, Herschel Grynszpan, angered by his parents' brutal expulsion from Germany, murdered Ernst von Rath, the third secretary of the German Embassy. A wave of destruction, looting, and firebombing of Jewish properties swept across Europe in retaliation. This event was called *Kristallnacht,* or "crystal night," for on that night, the shop windows of Jewish businesses throughout the country were broken by the Nazis, and synagogues were damaged. From then on, the persecution of the Jews ran rampant. Like a tidal wave, it soon rolled through the Ukraine, and the rest of the occupied territories, leaving fear and death behind.

In the spring of 1941, Theodor was walking along the sidewalk of the main boulevard in Kolomeya. As he attempted to cross the street, a Nazi officer blew his whistle, shouted in German, and stopped all traffic in the busy intersection. Down the middle of the street the Nazis led hundreds, perhaps thousands, of Jewish men who had been forced from their homes. The Jewish men, dressed in black overcoats and black hats, were heading to their own funeral. The men walked slowly as the Nazi officers yelled at them, prodding them to walk faster. The Jews knew where they were going.

The execution took place in a forest on the west side of Kolomeya, some three kilometers away. Theodor learned from the people who lived near the execution site about the long, massive graves in the forest. Some who took part in the execution bragged about how it was done. The Nazis forced the Jews to line up on the edge of the grave and then shot them from behind with machine guns. Then the Nazis and the Ukrainian police pushed the rest of them into the

---

* "World War II Casualties." Wikipedia, http://en.wikipedia.org/World_War_II_casualties#Casualties_by_country. (Accessed in August 2007.) In Poland, Holocaust deaths were calculated to be in the three millions, more than in any other European nation.

grave. Even those who were not mortally wounded were pushed in and then buried alive.

After arresting and killing all the Jewish men of Kolomeya, the Nazis forced the Jewish women and children, already living in the ghetto, to stay inside their houses. If any attempted to escape, they were shot. Then the Nazis hurled hand grenades into the houses, setting all the houses ablaze and burning the women and children inside. If anyone escaped, the Nazis simply threw them back into the fire.

The smoke of the ghetto fires billowed above Kolomeya, darkening the sky. Where Theodor and his family lived, five kilometers away, they could see the smoke and could smell the burned flesh for days.

Theodor's brother, Slawko, worked for a German medical unit and witnessed much of the brutality himself. At night he would return, ashen faced and sober, quietly debriefing the horrific scenes to his brother. After the ghetto had burned, a few Nazis remained behind to comb the area for anyone who might have escaped the fire. As the men were searching for escapees, they found a pretty, young Jewish girl hiding in a huge pillow. She pleaded for mercy, and the surprised Nazi wondered what to do with her. The Ukrainian policeman with him politely moved the SS man to the side, and to Slawko's horror, pulled out his own handgun and shot her. "He considered himself a big hero for that," Slawko choked. Theodor held his brother as he sobbed.

One early morning Theodor went to the city bakery to buy bread with ration stamps. Two Gestapo men, their uniforms grimy and their faces covered with soot, arrived for breakfast.

"Look at those poor, hardworking men," said the store owner to all who were waiting in line. "They were working all night in the ghetto." Most of the others in line murmured their sympathy and support. Theodor's stomach lurched. He looked down at the floor and silenced the indignation burning inside. No one dared to openly object to the Nazi system.

One evening, Caroline, Theodor's stepmother, received an official letter in the mail. Rarely did she ever receive her own mail, so she opened it with great curiosity, the entire family waiting. As she read it, her face became flushed.

"What is this?" she cried, waving the letter. "The German government says that because I have the maiden name of Miller, I must register as either a Jew or a German. My maiden name is unusual in this area, and it caught their attention."

"Do you know what nationality your name is?" asked Onofre.

"No!" said Caroline. "I have no idea. My parents have died, and they, too, knew nothing of their background. Personally, I've never cared to find out. What difference does it make?" She sat down, agitated, in a kitchen chair.

"Well," said Onofre, cautiously. "It makes a lot of difference to them. Look what they are doing to the Jews."

Theodor cringed. His brothers and sister who were old enough to understand looked ill.

"Does this mean that if your name is Jewish, they will kill you?" exclaimed Daria, color draining from her face.

"Not just her," said Onofre. "They'll kill the entire family. They don't want any taint of the Jewish race contaminating their bloodlines." Daria began to wail, and her younger brothers joined in.

"Yes, they state openly in the letter that if my heritage is Jewish, we will all suffer the fate of the Jews. If only it were just me." Tears poured down her cheeks.

"It's going to be OK," comforted Onofre. "God has always protected us. Let's stay calm and pray. When do they expect an answer?"

"As soon as possible. But I don't know what to tell them. I have no idea of what origin the name Miller is."

"Just say 'German' and be done with it," suggested Slawko. "That would solve all the problems."

"No, I just can't register us as German if I don't know," Caroline argued. "I don't want to involve us in any politics."

"You're right," said Onofre. "We should stay as neutral as we can. Why don't you write back and tell them you don't know. Maybe that will stall them for a while."

Caroline followed his advice, but the Gestapo was not satisfied. Again another letter arrived at their home stating tersely, "Find out."

Caroline waited a while and then replied. She couldn't track down any supporting references for her family line, she explained. There was no way to tell her ancestry. But the Gestapo still persisted. "You will have to make the decision yourself," they wrote back. If she would register as a *Volksdeutscher,* a person of German descent, the Pawluks' problem, for the time being, would be over. The family would enjoy all the privileges of being Germans. When Caroline still refused to commit, she and Onofre were called in several times for questioning.

One day Theodor's parents returned home from a meeting with the Gestapo, their faces graver than usual. "Theodor," they told their oldest, "we are sending you and all the children to your uncle's house for a few days."

"Why?" he asked, the familiar feeling of fear encircled him again.

"We are certain that the Gestapo may pick us up any night. We want to make sure you will be safe."

Theodor gulped.

"Please watch over the rest of your brothers and sister, will you?"

Theodor nodded.

After the Gestapo's threats, Onofre and Caroline realized that their hesitation was endangering the future of their eight children—whether they would continue to live on their farm or perish by fire in the ghetto—so they made their decision.

"We gave in," Caroline told Theodor a few days later when she and Onofre came to retrieve their anxious children.

"We're all going into town tomorrow morning to register as German citizens," Onofre announced to the family.

"Are you kidding?" exclaimed Theodor. "I'm not a German! Not after what I've seen them do."

"Better than dying as a Jew," Slawko reminded him.

"No," argued Theodor. "The oldest three children are not related to the Miller line. Since we're only your stepchildren, we can't be included," he told Caroline. "Slawko, Daria, and I are full-blooded Ukrainian."

"Well, suit yourself," said "Onofre. "But I don't think they'll leave you alone."

"I can't imagine they mean us too," Theodor insisted. "We have no Miller blood in us. I'm not going to go."

"I'm not either," said Slawko.

Daria said nothing. She wanted to stay with her parents.

"OK," Onofre shrugged. The next morning, Onofre, Caroline, and the rest of the six children entered the Gestapo office.

Volksdeutscher, they wrote, signing their way to safety.

"List number of sons," the citizenship form stated.

"Seven," they wrote. The Gestapo surveyed their completed documents.

"You have seven sons?" an official asked, counting the number of boys present.

"Yes," said Onofre.

"I count only five with you," the official said. "Where are the other two?"

"They're at home," Onofre replied. "They didn't feel they needed to come in, since they had a different mother."

"I see," said the official, raising his eyebrows. "But you are all a family unit." He paused to write himself a note. "Well, since you have more than three sons, you are now entitled to receive a monthly allowance from the German government." He pushed more papers across the desk for the Pawluks to sign.

Caroline's eyes brightened. This was a perk she hadn't anticipated. Maybe being a German citizen wouldn't be so bad, after all.

Another letter arrived at the Pawluk home, this time addressed to Theodor and Slawko.

"You must register with the Gestapo immediately," the letter ordered. Theodor groaned.

"I didn't think they would leave you alone," Onofre said.

"I guess not," said Theodor. "Looks like we have no choice."

Reluctantly the brothers rode into Kolomeya and went to the train station. There they entered the string of converted railroad wagons that composed the Nazi's offices. They were directed to the headquarters for registration.

"Have a seat," the Gestapo officer invited. He smiled warmly at the boys. "Let me ask you a few questions. Where were you born?"

Theodore found the questions fairly general and easy to answer. He was surprised at how friendly and kind the Gestapo was. It wasn't what he expected. After signing paper after paper and having their pictures taken, the boys were each handed an official German passport, a large black swastika emblazoned on the front.

"You now belong to the best race on earth," the official said with great aplomb. "This is a glory and an honor," he added, smiling broadly. "And as such, you are now entitled to all the benefits. Heil Hitler!" He saluted smartly.

"Heil Hitler," Theodor returned politely. Those words sounded strange to him, but as everyone seemed proud to be a German, it was difficult not to feel the same way. They exited the registration office, strangely excited.

"They didn't even ask us if we wanted to be Germans," Theodor commented.

"Wow! This is great!" Slawko said, waving his document proudly. "Wait until my friends see this. They are going to have to give me more respect now!"

Theodor just laughed at his brother, knowing Slawko would flash that passport like a silver badge. He, too, realized that he had gained an important status. It was hard always being scorned for being a Seventh-day Adventist, but now, becoming a German—this was another story.

"We won't be drafted into forced labor in Germany like the rest of the fellows our age," Theodor said. "If I had known this earlier, I wouldn't have been so reluctant to register."

Slawko agreed.

A few days later, Onofre received another letter from the government.

"Another letter," sighed Caroline. "What do they want from us now?" she asked.

"A farm," Onofre said.

"What!" cried Caroline. "But they told us we were entitled to all the privileges of a German citizen! Now they will take away our property?" She threw her dishtowel in frustration.

"Actually, they don't care about this farm, but they are ordering us to resettle an abandoned farm in Fleberg."

"Isn't Fleberg a German colony on the northwest side of Kolomeya?" asked Theodor. "Why do they want us to move there?"

"When the war started in 1941, the German farmers who lived in the Fleberg colony all moved to Germany, leaving their farms empty. The German officials now want us to resettle those deserted farms. We are German citizens now, after all."

"They're asking me to leave the farm where I was born?" cried Theodor. "I don't like that!"

"Apparently, this new farm is much larger than our own," continued Onofre, "and the property surrounds the farmhouse. Our fields right now are scattered all over the place. Just think of how much easier it will be to take care of the land."

"What will happen to this place?" Theodor asked.

"Nothing," his father said. "It will become just like other abandoned farmhouses."

"It doesn't matter," Caroline said. "We have no choice but to move. As long as we're all safe and together, I won't complain. Fleberg is as nice an area as any."

Theodor grumped in his chair. "I can take care of this farm by myself," he announced. "I'm not going anywhere."

"Aw, Theo," said Slawko. "It's just a farm."

"I'm old enough to manage this by myself," said Theodor.

He leaned forward in earnest. "Father, all I have to do is cultivate a small half-acre near the house for my own food, and I will be able to completely support myself. I'll keep the place up, and if you are ever forced to leave Fleberg, we will still have our farm. If we abandon it now, it will be gone forever."

Onofre twisted his mustache in thought.

"You have a point there," he said.

"What!" said Caroline. "You're giving in so quickly?"

"He's sixteen, Caroline, and old enough to start his own career, so he's old enough to have his own home," his father said. "He's responsible and hardworking. I know he can do it."

"All right," said Caroline, shaking her head. "But, Theodor, when will we ever see you?"

"Every week," said Theodor. "At church, of course, and every few weeks, I'll come to the new place to get some of your home cooking." He laughed, but secretly, he looked forward to a little peace and quiet after living in a house with seven rambunctious younger siblings.

*　*　*　*

For two years, Theodor stayed on the old farm, cultivating corn, potatoes, and other vegetables. He was a completely independent young man. The evenings were quiet, and when he didn't have a houseful of young companions from town (the Pawluk house soon became a popular hangout), he played hymns on the mandolin or read from his little Bible. Every week he saw his family at church, and, as promised, he visited them every other week at their new home.

One Christmas Day Theodor decided to go to the local Greek Orthodox church to see how they observed Christmas. At that time, Seventh-day Adventist churches did not hold Christmas programs because they considered Christmas a pagan holiday. His parents, consequently, treated the day as any other. Theodor, on the other hand, enjoyed the holiday and thought celebrating Jesus' birth was a grand thing to do, no matter what pagan tradition influenced the choice of the twenty-fifth as the day to celebrate. He always gave small presents to his brothers and sister on Christmas, though his parents and siblings never gave Theodor anything in return.

I have nothing else to do, he thought. *It won't hurt anybody if I just slip in and watch the Christmas program.* Making his way to his family's former church, he found a vacant pew and sat down to enjoy the service. Theodor enjoyed the choir, the preaching, the singing, and even the chanting. He tried unsuccessfully to remain inconspicuous.

"It's Theodor Pawluk," someone whispered loudly. "Look who's here! It's Onofre Pawluk's son." Theodor felt the eyes of interested villagers devouring him with excitement.

Uh-oh. What have I done? Theodor thought, squirming in his pew.

"The prodigal son is home!" "Theodor is returning to church!" "Has he been converted?" another member asked. Neighbors and former family friends swarmed him after the service. "Welcome back!" they said, hugging Theodor. Theodor awkwardly greeted the people who had wanted nothing to do with him or his family. Now it seemed he was the only one they thought worth noticing. Considering the Pawluk family to be heretics, the townspeople had either ignored or ridiculed the family for years. Theodor greeted the now-friendly people and quickly left.

"See you next Sunday," a member called. Theodor waved good-bye.

In town and wherever he went in the following days, Theodor remained the center of attention.

"Have you decided to return to us?" the people asked, expressing their pleasure.

"I just wanted to see your Christmas program," Theodor explained. "It was a beautiful service, and we don't have programs like that for Christmas in our church."

The villagers' faces darkened. "You mean you're not coming back?"

"Well, no. Maybe for another special program," he answered truthfully. "I'm still a Seventh-day Adventist. But I really enjoyed visiting again."

The warm looks and courteous treatment evaporated into icy glares. Old and young alike, men, women, and children all resumed their hostile behavior. When the next Sunday came and went and Theodor remained absent, the local Greek Orthodox members grew furious.

"If you don't come back to our church, you soon won't be going to any church again," someone warned.

"We'll get rid of you, Pawluk," another one threatened. "You think we're joking, but we're not." Realizing that he had stirred up the ire of the Kornich village, Theodor avoided the townspeople as much as he could.

One night soon after, as he lay in bed in the quiet farmhouse, he heard thumps and rattling at a window. Someone was trying to break in. As the sounds grew more insistent, Theodor threw on his clothes and his heavy winter coat and grabbed his Bible. He crept up the stairs to the attic and opened a trapdoor on the roof. As he crawled out into the chilly darkness, breaking glass shattered from a window in the house below. Climbing down the far side of the roof, he jumped to the ground and ran, forever leaving the farmhouse and the angry villagers of Kornich behind. Theodor fled to his parents' farm in Fleberg, almost twenty miles away.

"Theodor," said his father one morning as they worked together at the new farm, "it is time for the career discussion again. You are good at farming, and you know all about the weaving business, too; but is this what you want to do with the rest of your life?"

"No," said Theodor. "But after my plans for going into the ministry were canceled, I haven't given it much thought. I wanted to attend a Seventh-day Adventist college, but all of them are closed throughout Europe."

"I know," Onofre answered. "The schools are occupied by Germans or by the Allied armies. Who knows when they are going to leave and when the schools will be reopened. Isn't there another occupation you could choose, for the meantime, at least?"

"I don't know," Theodor said. "I know I want a profession that I can work at on my own, so I will never have any trouble getting the Sabbath off."

"How about tailoring?" suggested Onofre. "You're good with your hands."

"I do like working with fabric," said Theodor. "And I've always enjoyed sewing." Tailoring was a fashionable business in Europe, and the idea appealed to him. "And I do like nice clothing," Theodor added.

"Another advantage is that tailoring is done indoors," reminded his father. "You wouldn't be exposed to cold, snowy, and rainy days the way outdoor workers are." That aspect attracted Theodor, as well. Soon, he decided to follow Onofre's suggestion and became an apprentice to a tailor. Few things were more satisfying than seeing the happy faces of the customers as they tried on the new suits he had made.

As much as Theodor valued free enterprise, a welcome relief after the oppressive Communist regime, he loved even more the freedom to worship openly in his church once again. Because the four local Adventist churches had not been able to meet or associate together during the Soviet occupation, the churches planned a small, area-wide camp meeting to reconnect. However, wanting to remain inconspicuous, they chose the secluded village of White-Oslave in the Carpathian Mountains to hold their retreat. Large groups of people could still excite suspicion in the valley, and the majority of the population still held animosity for their Protestant faith.

One of the church members in White-Oslave owned a large farm with a spacious, grass-covered yard behind the house, perfect for such an outdoor gathering. The members chose this site for their camp meeting.

As it would have been difficult traveling with all the little ones in the family, Onofre decided to stay home with the children. Theodor and Caroline would make the overnight trip and represent the family. Theodor and his mother rolled up their quilts and pillows and set out with great anticipation. There were no tents, but they would sleep comfortably in the church member's barns.

Most of the campers arrived by Friday noon. Theodor and Caroline visited with church members and friends until the evening. There was so much catching up to do.

"How did God protect you during the Communist regime?" they asked each other. In sharing, they discovered that many of their members had been arrested by the Soviets for their faith and had disappeared. No one knew what had happened to them. As the sun dipped in the west, the members gathered in the large farmhouse to welcome the Sabbath with a devotional service. More and more people arrived until there was barely standing room.

Sabbath dawned as bright as the hearts of the reunited friends and church families. They planned to praise God with singing and praying and then have an hour of testimonies, sharing how God had cared for His people in their times of trouble. The Adventist conference had sent several ordained ministers to preach. This would be a treat. By eleven o'clock Sabbath morning, such a large crowd had assembled that there was not enough room inside the house.

"Let's hold the service outside under that large, spreading tree," someone suggested. The people filed out into the warm breeze and sunshine, arranging themselves on the grass in the shade.

As their songs carried through the open air, two armed Ukrainian policemen walked up to the group and settled themselves politely with the other worshipers. Theodor flinched. *Why are they here?* he wondered. *It was all going so well.* Others around him fidgeted, casting sidelong glances at the two officers.

"Maybe they just want to hear a good sermon," Caroline whispered to him.

"That's unlikely," Theodor whispered back. A new tension settled over the entire congregation. The service that had begun with anticipation now carried the weight of suspense. *What will happen next?* everyone wondered.

When the visiting minister addressed the crowd, he carried on naturally, praising God and exhorting all of them to continue serving God, no matter what happened. He talked about the second coming of Christ and last-day events. Life had already been a time of trouble and persecution for most of the assembly, so the message resonated powerfully.

" 'Ye shall be hated of all men for my name's sake,' " the pastor quoted, " 'but he that shall endure unto the end, the same shall be saved.' "*

Theodor thought of his own experiences. He knew already what it was like to be despised and rejected, a consequence of following God.

" 'Be careful for nothing,' " the pastor encouraged, reading from Philippians. " 'But in every thing by prayer and supplication with thanksgiving let your requests be made known unto God. And the peace of God, which passeth all understanding, shall keep your hearts and minds through Christ Jesus.' "†

What is it like to have this kind of peace? Theodor pondered. It was one thing to be inspired by God's promises and testimonies about God's deliverance through the terrible days behind them, but quite another to be at peace when the police, with an unknown agenda, sat nearby. Throughout the sermon, the two Ukrainian officers listened quietly, as if they were soaking it in. *Maybe they really are just curious,* Theodor hoped. *They probably just want to see what such a large crowd is up to in this place.*

The congregation sang a closing hymn, and the pastor gave the closing prayer. Immediately after the benediction, the policemen

---

* Mark 13:13.
† Philippians 4:6, 7.

stood up and walked forward to the front. Theodor's stomach growled with hunger.

"All men present are under arrest," one police officer announced. Gasps could be heard throughout the crowd. Then all was quiet. Theodor looked around at the other men, some trying to comfort their wives and children. He realized that he was the youngest man there.

I wish my father were here! he thought, longing for the quiet assurance of his father's presence.

"Please follow us to the police station," the officer continued. "All the women must remain here." The men and women looked at each other in distress. One officer picked his way through the crowd and waited for the men to file after him. The other waved the men on from the back. Caroline grabbed Theodor's arm.

"I'd really rather have lunch," whispered Theodor to his mother, "but I think Satan has another plan." The men began filing behind the leading officer. The second officer stayed behind, ensuring that all complied.

"Let's get moving," the officer at the end ordered to those who moved too slowly. "I'm going with you," Caroline whispered.

"You can't," Theodor argued, hoping she would.

"I won't let you go alone." She held tightly to Theodor's arm as they joined the men trailing behind the police.

The men, and Caroline, followed the police down the dirt road into the middle of the little village. There at the police station, the officers herded the group of about seventy men into the courtyard. "Wait here," they ordered. A few extra police, standing with guns ready, guarded against escape attempts.

"You," one officer called to a man in the front. "Follow me." The man followed the policeman into the office, the door closing behind them. After a few minutes, another man was called, then another. Theodor and Caroline watched anxiously for the church members to return, but no one did. Another man was called.

"I wonder why the men aren't coming out?" Theodor asked, feeling sick. "There is not that much room inside the police station for all of us." Caroline's head was down, praying. She didn't answer. Theodor was too frightened to pray.

What's going to happen will happen, thought Theodor grimly. *What can God do?* He sulked in his worry, trying to have the faith of his mother, some kind of peace, but failing miserably.

"You," a policeman said, pointing finally at Theodor. "Come in." Caroline squeezed his arm before she let go. Theodor shuffled after the official into the office. The officer walked over to the small desk stacked with papers and grabbed a pen. Theodor waited.

"Name?" the man snapped.

"Theodor Pawluk."

"Address?" Theodor replied, one step ahead, while fishing out his identification papers. He held out his German passport.

The officer, busy writing, waved the papers away without looking up. Theodor replaced his passport in his coat jacket. "Step over to the other room," the man commanded, waving toward a door on the far side of the small office. Theodor obeyed.

As he turned the knob and stepped inside, light beamed into a corner, revealing an otherwise pitch-dark room. Confused, Theodor turned around again. *Is there a mistake? Maybe I didn't understand him right.* He stood at the entrance, looking back at the officer, uncertain what to do.

"Close the door," a rough voice yelled at him in German from inside. Theodor jumped, stepped into the room, and shut the door, his heart pounding. "Come here," the voice ordered. As his eyes adjusted to the darkness, he could make out a table and two German soldiers. They were waiting beside the table, each holding upraised clubs.

"Take off your clothes," one soldier commanded. Theodor could smell the stench of whiskey heavy on his breath. Theodor stared at them and slowly began to unbutton his shirt.

Chapter 7

Theodor stood in front of the large table in the darkness, his legs wobbling.

"Lie facedown on the table," barked the soldier.

Sickened, Theodor finished unbuttoning his shirt. "Hurry up," the soldier growled. Theodor pulled off his clothes and dropped them to the floor. *Help!* he could only pray. Placing his hand on the table, Theodor felt something wet and sticky. Flinching, he climbed up.

Suddenly the door flew open, spilling light over his bare skin, outlining his skinny back and revealing the soldiers with lifted clubs.

"Don't touch him! He is a German citizen," the policeman at the door shouted.

"What!" exclaimed one of the soldiers, cursing under his breath.

"Put your clothes back on and leave the room," the other soldier said brusquely. "That way." He pointed to a door on the far side of the chamber. Theodor never dressed himself so quickly in his whole life. The door slammed shut behind him, leaving the soldiers back in the darkness.

Thank You, God, Theodor prayed, exiting into warm daylight. He blinked. The church members were not there, nor his mother.

He had been let out another way. A guard showed him to the gate in the courtyard fence, unlocked it, and Theodor stepped out into a quiet alley.

I guess I'll go back to the camp meeting, he thought. *My mother must be waiting for me there.* Returning to the farm, Theodor kept wondering at his sudden deliverance. *God answered my mother's prayers,* he thought. *I was too busy being afraid to pray.*

" 'The effectual fervent prayer of a righteous man availeth much,' "* he quoted. Then he shuddered, thinking of the other church members before him and those still waiting in line. He didn't want to think of what was happening to them.

When he reached the camp meeting, Caroline welcomed him with tears of joy. "Thank God, you're not hurt," she cried. She had returned to the farm only a few minutes ahead of him.

"How did they know I was a German citizen?" he asked her. "Did you tell them?"

"Yes," she said. "A minute after you went in, I barged into the office and informed the police officer that you were German. You had already gone inside the other room."

"Why did that stop them from beating me?" he asked.

"Don't you remember that the German government passed a law prohibiting foreigners from hurting a German citizen? According to that law, the German authorities would take ten Ukrainians out of the prison and execute them for hurting you."

"I guess it is handy to be a German citizen," Theodor said. "But what about the other men? What happened to the men ahead of me? Are they here?" Theodor looked around. Most of the women still waited, hands clasped, looking down the road Theodor had just walked.

"They're inside the house," Caroline said. "They've been beaten up badly."

* James 5:16.

"But am I the only one to escape the beatings?" Theodor asked, chagrined. He thought of his own lack of trust. "Why me?" Caroline shook her head.

"The apostle Paul was in the same predicament when he was arrested," she said. "When they were going to whip him, Paul asked the centurion, 'Is it lawful for you to scourge a man that is a Roman?' And they didn't whip him."*

"But no one else here deserved to be beaten," Theodor mourned. "I don't understand."

"I know, but you're the youngest man here, if you had been clubbed like they were, there wouldn't be much left of you," Caroline smiled, hugging his slender frame.

Inside the house, Theodor saw the wives of the injured men washing the bloody wounds and bruises with warm water. There was no way of getting medical help. For several hours, beaten, bleeding men limped up the road, one by one. Some were singing, despite their pain. The waiting believers hoped and prayed that all would return.

Miraculously they did. When all the wounds were bandaged, following a belated lunch, camp meeting resumed with a long testimony and praise period that Theodor would never forget.

" 'All that will live godly in Christ Jesus shall suffer persecution,' "† one beaten man said.

" 'And if we suffer, we shall also reign with him,' "§ praised another member. Over and over, the members shared their faith in the Scriptures and how God had been with them through their trials. Theodor didn't have much to say, though he knew God had been with him too. But he absorbed it all, his young heart full of gratitude and longing. How he wanted a faith like they had, all the more strengthened through suffering.

The camp meeting ended and Theodor and his mother returned

---

* Acts 22:25–27.
† 2 Timothy 3:12.
§ 2 Timothy 2:12.

home. "Why did they beat us?" Theodor asked. "We weren't doing anything wrong." The mystery was solved when church members in White-Oslave later learned about the local priest's role in the persecution and informed the church members in the three other villages.

"When the local village priest found out about the camp meeting, he became angry," the messenger told them. "He went to the local police to ask them to stop the camp meeting, but they wouldn't help him. It is illegal for the Ukrainian police to beat civilians; only Germans are allowed to. Taking the matter into his own hands, the priest flagged down a military vehicle containing German soldiers traveling on a nearby highway.

" 'In my village, there is a big gathering of people who keep the Jewish Sabbath,' the priest said. 'Would you help us disperse them?' He then offered the soldiers money and whiskey for beating up the Adventists. The German soldiers willingly accepted the bribe and forced the Ukrainian police to assist them."

* — * — * — *

As everything in this world has its beginning and its end, so did the Nazi Empire. It had promised and planned to be a thousand-year *Reich,* and in its beginning, with all its might and power, it looked as though it might last forever. But the Third Reich lasted only eleven years and seven months; even the Fuhrer himself had a miserable end.

The German Empire started to crumble at Stalingrad in December of 1942. Just as Napoleon Bonaparte could not survive the Russian winter, which in some places reached fifty to sixty degrees below zero, so, too, the Nazis failed. Because the Germans expected to take Stalingrad in another *Blitzkrieg,* employing tactics similar to those that had been successful in the German occupation of western Europe, they did not plan to wage war during the winter. But this time the Germans met significant resistance.

Another factor contributing to the Nazi defeat was that the United States supplied the Soviets with military hardware they needed, and, as a result, the German army lost three hundred thousand men in the Battle of Stalingrad. That defeat at Stalingrad is considered the turning point of the war in the eastern front, and the Germans never recovered. Following that defeat, the Germans lost ground so quickly that within a few months the Soviets were on their way back to the Ukraine.

The Pawluk family received the news with great alarm.

"The Russians are coming back!" Theodor announced to his parents and younger siblings.

"Not again!" cried Daria. "Will you have to join the collective farm again, Theo?"

"I think we've got worse problems than that to think about," said Theodor.

"What do you mean?" Daria asked. "How can it be harder than it was before?"

"We're now the enemy," he answered, concern showing on his face. Onofre nodded, his face also grave.

"I knew changing our citizenship would spell trouble," mourned Caroline. "But we didn't have a choice."

"I don't understand," Daria wailed. "This is still our country."

"We're German now," Slawko shot back. "With all their privileges, remember? And now it's the Germans' privilege to run for their lives."

"What will happen to us?" asked Daria. She hugged a clinging younger brother in her arms.

"God will take care of us," Onofre reassured, "but we do need to take some action. The act of changing our citizenship from Russian to German, joining the enemy of the Soviet Union, will be considered an act of high treason. They won't let this fact escape them." Onofre paced the kitchen floor.

"And the fact that we lived under their government before and knew their system so well doesn't help," Slawko pointed out.

"Right," Theodor muttered. "As 'Germans' we can't welcome them home; they'll consider us turncoats."

"Well, aren't we?" asked Slawko cynically. "It won't matter that it wasn't our choice."

"No," said Onofre. He put his hand on his forehead and rubbed his eyebrows. Caroline picked up a kitchen pot and started scrubbing.

"What happens to traitors?" asked Daria.

"Nothing good—" began Theodor.

"Execution or deportation to Siberia," Slawko blurted.

"Stop it," Caroline ordered, but the tremor in her voice showed that she understood and agreed with Slawko's assessment. They all knew the truth. Onofre walked over to his wife and hugged her. She rested her head on his shoulder for a moment but then straightened. "Onofre," she said. "We can't leave the farm. Everything we have is here—our animals, grain, vegetables, milk . . ." her voice trailed into a sob.

"We have to leave," he said. "There's no other way."

"I make cheese and butter from the milk," Caroline said, wiping her eyes. Daria stared at her parents in alarm.

"We have to leave?" she whispered.

"Yes," her father answered, turning to his children. Theodor and Slawko tensed in their chairs. "We have to flee. We must leave behind our farm, our cattle, and everything that we have harvested and join the refugees going to Germany."

"There are thousands of them," said Theodor. "I just never thought we would be part of the group."

"Let's hope that the Soviets will not get so far west," his father added.

"We never have a choice," sighed Caroline. "We never have a choice."

"Who will take care of all the animals?" asked Daria. "Who will feed them?" No one had an answer. Theodor shook his head at her sadly.

"It's always one thing or another, isn't it?" Caroline said, brushing her hair back and straightening her shoulders. "OK, Onofre," she said resolutely. "What's the plan?"

"We need to start getting ready," he said. "We may still have a few months before the Russians arrive."

"It will take a while to get food ready for the trip," Caroline said. "We need to bake a lot of bread, slice it, and dry it thoroughly to preserve it. We have a lot of work to do."

"In the meantime, we'll listen to the news and keep track of how close the Russians are getting," Onofre said.

Theodor watched his stepmother, the only mother he had ever known. How he loved her. He would never forget how she stayed by his side when he had been arrested at the camp meeting, even though the women were told to stay behind. Her courage, in spite of the circumstances, always inspired him, especially how she rallied to whatever task was at hand. It was hard to see her heartbroken. But even now, heading into the unknown, she carried herself with quiet confidence.

"We can't all go by horse and wagon," Onofre said. "When it's time to leave, I think it best that you and the children travel on ahead by train. The German government has provided one for the refugees. Theodor and I will follow with the wagon." Caroline nodded. Already she headed off to begin make preparations for the journey.

In Matthew 24:20, Jesus told His followers to "pray ye that your flight be not be in the winter neither on the sabbath day." The Pawluks had never thought seriously of this text applying to them, though Theodor remembered reading the text many times. Nevertheless, it was on the Sabbath day, several months later, that the news came. The Russians were too close to ignore any longer. It was time to leave their home and head for a place of safety. In winter, February of 1944, the family began their long trek to Germany.

When the truck came to take Caroline and the children, who were all bundled for warmth against the cold, to the train station,

Caroline had disappeared. No one could find her. She was not in the house, the cellar, the attic, or in the fields around the farm.

"Where could she have gone?" Theodor asked.

"I'll check the barn," Onofre said. He found her in the stable, hugging the cow's neck, crying. "You gave us all the milk we needed," Caroline crooned through her tears, petting the black-splotched neck. "We have to go now." The cow, its wide eyes blinking, switched its tail in reply. Reluctant to say the last goodbye, Caroline kept her hold around the cow's neck until Onofre gently pried her away.

"The truck is leaving," he said. Theodor watched his father guide his mother to the truck, her face wet with tears. After more hurried goodbyes, the truck rumbled down the driveway. *When will we see them again?* Theodor wondered. He tried to swallow the lump in his throat.

"Do we really have to leave the animals in the barn?" asked Theodor, hitching up the horse to the wagon. "They're sure to starve to death in there."

"Why don't we set them loose in the open fields?" his father suggested, adjusting the reins of the horse. He stroked the animal's soft face. "Perhaps they will be able to forage for food there. Their chances of survival will be greater on their own."

"You're right," Theodor agreed. "That's what I was thinking too. But it won't be long before the Soviet army shows up."

However many of the animals might survive on their own, Theodor knew that after the Soviet army descended upon them, many would be either slaughtered for food or else cruelly used as targets. Theodor remembered reading the words of the prophet Jeremiah: "How long shall the land mourn, and the herbs of every field wither, for the wickedness of them that dwell therein? the beasts are consumed, and the birds; because they said, He shall not see our last end."* He gritted his teeth.

---

* Jeremiah 12:4.

After freeing the animals, Onofre and his son loaded the wagon with clothing and preserved food and then set out on their long journey toward Germany. They stopped first in the village of Fleberg, where all the men from the German settlement, some two hundred in number, gathered in the school auditorium to organize and to receive instructions on the way to go and whom to follow. There were no women in the group, because they had been sent ahead by train. There was much confusion there, but fortunately, the German authorities had assigned a former military commander, currently on leave from the war, to take charge.

The SS-Oberscharführer* was a middle-aged man, with blond hair, blue eyes, and a clean-shaven face. He had served in the elite SS unit with a rank of a lieutenant. During the war, SS troops had been utilized to break through enemy lines too fortified for the regular infantry. SS soldiers were known for their skilled and ruthless killing and for their fearless willingness to plow through anyone or anything in their path.

Standing with the others alongside one wall of the auditorium, Theodor listened to the advice and warnings from their new leader. He told them how to line up for duty and how the journey would proceed.

"I will be riding on a motorcycle, driving back and forth, keeping track of where the Soviet army is. I will tell you when to stop and when to start. You will all get weapons," he said, "and everyone will guard our group in shifts throughout the night when we stop to rest."

He pointed to a pile of guns and ammunition in the center of the hall. "Everyone needs a rifle," the SS-Oberscharführer continued. "You will also need enough ammunition for your protection against the guerrilla fighters. There are many hostile Ukrainians in the villages who may try to slow our progress." Theodor liked the thought of having his own gun. As the men were handed their weapons, he

---

* A rank similar to senior company leader or senior squad leader.

beamed, stroking the shiny barrel and wooden shaft with pleasure. Onofre, on the other hand, having fought in a war himself, showed no such delight.

"It's nothing to be happy about, Theo," he said, his voice reflective. "A gun isn't what will keep you safe." Theodor looked up at his father.

"You're probably right," Theodor answered. "But it makes me feel more in control." His father turned away with a sad smile on his face.

"Hey, Theodor," yelled a voice from the other side of the auditorium. Theodor looked up to see a neighbor about his age jokingly aiming a rifle directly at him.

"Quit it," barked Theodor. "That's not funny."

"It's not loaded," returned the neighbor. "See." The boy pulled the trigger, and an explosion of gunpowder split the air. Standing nearby, Onofre turned in time to see Theodor crumpling like a rag doll to the floor.

Chapter 8

"N o," shrieked Onofre, rushing to his son's side. Everyone in the auditorium came running. The young man who shot the rifle turned white, guilt and terror contorting his face.

"I didn't know, I didn't know," he cried.

"Theodor," shouted his father, grabbing him, certain he was dead. "Theodor!" Theodor groaned and sat up, rubbing one ear with his hand. "I'm OK," he said. Murmurs of relief swept through the circle around him. "I felt the bullet singe my hair, and the blast knocked me over, but I'm OK."

"The bullet hit right here," someone announced, pointing at a bullet puncture in the wall, right where Theodor had been standing. "It missed his head by less than an inch!" Theodor winced.

Onofre hugged his son. "God must have something for you to do, Theo," he said. "It's a miracle you weren't killed." Theodor nodded. The rifle on the floor no longer seemed so appealing.

After receiving their instructions that Saturday night, Onofre, Theodor, and the rest of the German refugees from Fleberg clopped out of town. Setting out on the long journey, they joined the thousands of other refugee carts and wagons creaking over the cold roads.

The Theodor Pawluk Story

On March 29, 1944, after two years, nine months, and seven days of the German occupation, the Soviets returned to Kolomeya. The Pawluks had escaped just one month ahead of the Soviets' arrival.

The refugees rode for several days through the hills of the Ukraine. Theodor and his father took turns sleeping in the back of the wagon while the horses plodded onward. They stopped to rest by the side of the road at night. When they came to another small city, they stopped to give the horses a short rest.

While the refugees rested, soldiers from the German army stationed nearby approached their group. "We have a large military supply center here," the soldiers said, "but we have to abandon it. Instead of leaving everything for the Soviets, you people are welcome to take whatever you can use for yourselves."

Theodor and his father rummaged through the storehouse. Most of the supplies had already been taken or claimed. While poking around, though, something caught their eye, or rather, their stomachs.

"Sugar cubes!" said Theodor.

"We can use those," Onofre agreed. They lugged six fifty-kilogram bags of white sugar cubes to their wagon. Before this, they would soak the dried bread they had prepared in warm water. That had been their meal three times a day. Now adding sugar to their soggy bread, the food tasted much better.

They pushed onward for several days. But soon the first Soviet planes began swooping down over the trail of refugees. Many people were killed and many others injured. There was nothing to do but help the wounded and push on. Sporadically, the Soviet planes dropped bombs in addition to strafing with machine-gun fire. It was especially hazardous when the road lay exposed between open farmlands.

One evening the refugees from Fleberg came to a large pasture surrounded by forest, with room enough for the entire group to feed the horses. The SS-Oberscharführer gave the order to stop.

Other refugee groups had gathered in the pasture, as well. As Theodor set up camp with his father, he heard a baby crying in one of the groups. Nearby, he overheard the mother complaining to another woman.

"I wish I could find some sugar for my baby's food," she said. "But there's none anywhere." Theodor stopped short.

"Sugar?" he inquired, interrupting their conversation. "If you need sugar, follow me to my wagon." The surprised mother followed Theodor.

"Hold out your apron," he instructed. Then, lifting a sack of sugar, he poured the cubes into her apron—as much as she could carry.

"Oh my . . ." she said, stammering with shock and delight.

"Now, go and feed your baby," Theodor said, grinning. Smiling and grateful, the woman returned to her baby.

The Fleberg group left this oasis, continuing on their way. Eventually, Theodor's band arrived at a large village high in the Carpathian Mountains. The icy March wind chilled the travelers. With temperatures close to thirty degrees below zero, Theodor shivered in his long coat. He looked forward to warming himself by a fire that night.

But his hopes were dashed as angry shouts rang out in the evening air. Theodor tensed as threats and curses in Ukrainian echoed toward their wagons. "You filthy Germans stay out of our village," he heard. The SS-Oberscharführer and his assistant passed through the group.

"The people here are very hostile toward German citizens," they warned. "Don't knock on any doors. You must get out your guns and stand guard tonight, in case we are attacked."

Theodor groaned. So much for a warm fire. The night, spent outside on the village streets, would be long and cold. All the men stood on full alert, stamping their feet to keep warm. Theodor dutifully held his post next to his father, but even in his warm coat, he couldn't stop from shivering. "My toes hurt," he complained.

"Climb in the wagon and cover up with more blankets," his father told him. "You need to get warm."

"I need to stay at my post," Theodor said.

"No, you are younger and thinner than the rest of the men," Onofre insisted. "You need to get warm. Go climb in and cover up." Theodor obeyed and sat with his gun in the back of the wagon, but still he shivered.

As the night grew colder, Theodor's shivering grew uncontrollable. He took his feet out of his boots and rubbed his toes through his heavy socks. "My toes are numb," he mumbled. Onofre began to worry.

"How are you doing?" he asked Theodor again a while later.

"I'm OK," said Theodor sleepily. He no longer felt cold, though his face and lips were turning blue. "My feet don't hurt anymore. I'm getting more comfortable."

"You're getting hypothermia," Onofre stated. "You can't sit here in the cold any longer. We must warm you up."

"But how?" Theodor asked drowsily.

"I'm going to knock on one of those doors."

"But they hate us," Theodor began.

"They hate Germans," Onofre said, "but we're full-blooded Ukrainian. Have you forgotten?"

Theodor grunted.

"We'll leave our guns here," advised his father, hiding their weapons underneath the blankets.

"What if we need them? These people are dangerous."

"We've got the Sword of the Spirit," said Onofre, pulling out a small, worn Bible. "What more do we need?"

Theodor shook his head uneasily.

"Come on, then." Taking Theodor by the hand, Onofre tugged his son along, marching up to a nearby door. He knocked.

A villager cautiously opened the door, the man's face hardened with suspicion and hate. "Leave us alone," the man growled.

"My son is freezing to death," Onofre explained in his native tongue. Startled to hear Ukrainian rather than German, the man's face softened.

"Could we please come in and warm ourselves for a while?" Onofre begged.

"Come in," said the man. Theodor followed his father into the small living room and made a beeline for the fireplace. The villager offered each of them a chair. While Theodor warmed by the fire, Onofre pulled out his Bible and began leafing through it.

The villager and his family stared at Onofre in silence, surprised and curious. They had rarely seen a Bible, let alone had one in their home.

"What do you have there?" the man asked.

"Good news," Onofre said. "Would you like to hear what the Bible says about the future of this world? Did you know that the Bible predicted long ago that Hitler would never gain world supremacy?" He thumbed his Bible open to the book of Daniel.

"Really?" asked the man. "Please explain."

Onofre began to speak about the end of the world.

"Just a minute," the man said, "I've got to get some of my neighbors to hear this." He disappeared and returned a few minutes later with his friends. It wasn't long until the house was filled with neighbors wanting to hear the Word of God.

Beginning with the second chapter of Daniel, Onofre read the story of Nebuchadnezzar and his dream of the giant image. Point by point, he explained the fascinating prophecy; it was a good subject for a time like this.

"The prophecy points out very plainly that there will be only four world empires: Babylon, Media-Persia, Greece, and Rome," Onofre said. "No others."

"Hitler hasn't read that," said the villager.

"Well, yes," corrected Onofre gently. "One time we heard he was actually confronted with this prophecy. His response reportedly was, 'But where is the place for the Third Reich?' He's learning this the hard way." The listeners nodded.

"Later on," Onofre continued, "just as the Bible prophesied, Rome was divided into the ten kingdoms of Europe. The next world kingdom will be the kingdom of heaven, which shall never pass away. This is the kingdom we all want to have a part of."

On and on, Theodor listened to his father explain the Scriptures. The people could not get enough of it. They sat around talking and asking questions until two o'clock in the morning. Eventually, their host brought out some blankets, inviting Onofre and Theodor to sleep by the fire for a few hours.

Early in the morning the call came that the refugees must be on their way. The neighbors returned to see Onofre and Theodor off.

"Do you have to leave so soon?" they asked. "We want to hear more from the Bible."

"I wish we could stay," Onofre replied, reluctant to leave. Several families gave them gifts of fresh bread, eggs, butter, and cheese. Some even followed Onofre and Theodor, asking more and more questions, before finally turning back to their village.

"I wish we could spend more time with these people," Onofre told Theodor. "We will pray that they find a Bible and continue to study on their own."

Their journey soon brought relief from the bitter cold as they descended from the top of the Carpathian Mountains into a warmer climate. After a week, the refugees arrived at a deserted German colony. The German settlers who lived there had already fled to Germany, leaving their village a dark and quiet ghost town. Although large trees and green plants lured them to stay, the travelers discovered that this place, too, was a dangerous spot to linger. Some of the refugees who camped there before them had been ambushed by the Ukrainian partisans.

When Theodor started the journey, there were thousands, maybe millions, of refugees. But in order to not congest the road and to avoid Russian air force bombardments, the refugee groups had been divided, and each group was sent a different way. Onofre and

Theodor's group had dwindled to approximately one hundred men. In this dangerous place, Theodor wished there were more.

Though small, their group, thanks to the SS-Oberscharführer and his assistant, was well-organized. Every evening all the men lined up for duty and received the secret code for that night. Half the group would sleep, while the other half stood guard.

One night, about 3:00 A.M., as Theodor and another man stood watch at the empty colony, hidden behind a tree, Theodor's companion fell asleep. Suddenly, in the darkness, Theodor heard footsteps crunching through the leaves outside the camp, coming right toward him. It was too late to wake his fellow guard.

"Ask for the code first," they had been told. "If no one answers, then open fire." Theodor edged the safety off his weapon, waiting for just a few seconds longer before asking for the code. Just then, the target turned the other way. He breathed a prayer of thanks. God had spared his life—and someone else's.

The next evening, as the men lined up to receive their assignments, an unusual noise erupted from the last empty house down the road.

"Go check out that sound," the SS-Oberscharführer commanded Theodor and a companion. "We'll cover you at a distance." Theodor nodded.

In the darkness, Theodor and the other man slipped over to the house. The officer permitted no candles or flashlights because of the threat of air attacks, so the two entered the empty house in darkness.

"Who's there?" Theodor called out, fingering the rifle's trigger. "Surrender." His voice echoed in the empty rooms. No one answered. A dark attic hole opened above them on the far side of the room, but there was no ladder.

Unwilling to investigate each room in the total blackness, they decided to leave. Then Theodor heard it again. That strange scuffling sound. He spun back so quickly that his finger inadvertently pressed the trigger. The explosion ricocheted through the house, tearing away the thick silence covering the town. Leaping out of the doorway, Theodor and his friend waited for answering gunfire. There was only silence. They hurried back to camp with nothing to report. Again, the SS-Oberscharführer commanded the men to stand guard on full alert for the rest of the night.

In those places where the refugees were camped, there was nothing for Theodor and the others to do except wait for the command to go on. They did have to care for their horses, but this was simple as there was plenty of green grass where the horses could graze. All Theodor had to do was to stand and watch them.

One sunny Saturday morning, Theodor planned, for a change, to take his Bible to some quiet place and read it all day long, enjoying a special Sabbath retreat.

As Theodor set out to find a secluded spot, his Bible tucked away in his inner coat, the SS-Oberscharführer approached, his assistant a few paces behind.

"Heil Hitler," Theodor saluted as he passed them. He kept walking.

"Theodor," called the officer, "go cut some grass for my horses." Theodor stopped in his tracks, dread filling him. "While you are at it," the officer continued, "clean them up."

Theodor swallowed. He had been lucky, so far, to keep the Sabbath without confrontation. Taking a deep breath, he slowly turned around.

"Sir," Theodor said, deliberately, "I would be happy to do this for you, but today is the Sabbath." The SS-Oberscharführer stared at Theodor in disbelief. "Any other day, I would do this immediately for you, but the Bible says that no work should be done on the Sabbath day." There, he had said it. Theodor waited in dread for the officer's response.

The SS-Oberscharführer's face turned crimson with anger. "You dare to disobey an officer?" the man shouted, yanking his club out of its pouch. "What kind of nonsense is this?"

Theodor involuntarily stepped back. The SS-Oberscharführer's assistant sprang into action. Before Theodor could get away, the two men grabbed him and began to beat him—on his head, his face, his back—anywhere they could land a good swing on him. Theodor twisted and struggled, shielding himself with his hands as best he could. Eventually, wresting himself from their strong arms, Theodor tore away and ran, his body covered with bruises.

"That will teach you to disobey an officer," the men called after him. "If you ever speak to us like that again, you won't have the chance to run away."

Theodor hid out in an empty barn for the rest of the day, surrounding himself with old, dry hay. After surveying the damage to his swollen body, he pulled out his little Bible. *I guess I'll get to read my Bible after all,* Theodor thought to himself. *But what a price.* Turning its pages, Theodor was amazed at how meaningful reading his Bible could be after an experience like this. "Love your enemies . . ." he read. "Pray for them which despitefully use you, and persecute you."* Theodor dreaded the thought of seeing the SS-Oberscharführer again at roll call that evening, but there would be no way to avoid him. But emerging from the barn as the sun set, Theodor felt strengthened to endure another week. He would respect his leader as if nothing had happened. He would practice loving his enemies.

The SS-Oberscharführer ignored Theodor that evening and for the rest of the trip. He, too, acted as if the brutal beating had never happened. It was as if Theodor did not exist.

After camping in that one spot for almost a month, Theodor's group resumed their journey to Germany. He wasn't sad to leave that deserted colony behind. Because of constant air attacks, the group never traveled through cities or villages anymore. Soon they would be out of the mountains and out of the forest. Springtime was coming and the roads were dry. They picked up the pace, averaging nearly thirty-five kilometers per day.

Little progress could be made when the refugees had started the journey, two months earlier. Not only did thousands of refugees

---

* Matthew 5:44.

clog the road, many disguised Soviet agents mingled and merged with the refugee groups, pretending that they, too, were refugees, running from the Communists. These secret agents worked constantly to slow the progress of the travelers. For example, driving fully loaded trucks to a bridge or narrow passageway, the supposed refugees would purposefully disable the trucks.

"Our truck broke down," they would complain, putting forth little effort to move the barrier. In this way, the Soviet agents blocked traffic for hours, sometimes even for a day, hoping to help the Russians to catch up to the refugees.

Capture by the Communists was no idle threat. Not all the refugees escaped. Theodor learned that in some flat areas, far from the mountains and with little German resistance, the Communists overran throngs of refugees with devastating effects.

A few more weeks of travel behind them, Theodor's group again looked for a suitable place to rest themselves and their horses, a place with enough grass and water. This could only be found in farming country. Coming to a large flat area with adequate pastures for grazing, the group decided to pitch camp.

In this fertile country, the people were friendly and sympathetic to the refugees' plight. The farmers, themselves, were concerned about their own future, knowing that the approaching Communists disapproved of the region's free-enterprise system. They knew that the Communist government would take away their private land, forcing the collective farming method on them. To the farmers in the area, the refugees' arrival was a harbinger of the woes to come. But it looked as though the refugees were going to stay for a while. The farmers still had a reprieve.

"Why don't you come have Easter dinner with us?" a local farmer invited Onofre and Theodor a short time after the refugees had taken up residence. They gladly accepted. Perceiving that the Pawluks were God-fearing people, the host asked Onofre to say a few words about the resurrection of Christ and to have prayer at dinner.

Unaware of any Seventh-day Adventist believers in the area, Theodor and his father went through the village one Sunday looking for a church to attend. As they were passing by one house, they heard people singing church hymns, so Onofre and Theodor went to the door.

"Please come in," the people invited. During prayer time, Theodor grew uneasy. The volume of the people's prayers grew louder and louder. As the people knelt, they began to sway and moan. It appeared to him that the people were getting out of control. Theodor had never seen anything like it. In time, the wild praying simmered down and the pastor started to preach.

"Please stay for lunch," the congregation invited Theodor and his father after the service. "And would you preach for our afternoon service?" they asked Onofre. Onofre looked at his son. Theodor couldn't believe the invitation.

"Certainly," Onofre replied. "It would be my pleasure."

The group divided for lunchtime. One group took Onofre; the other group took Theodor. When Theodor saw that pork was being offered as the main course, he groaned inwardly.

"Would you ask God's blessing on the food?" they invited him. Again Theodor hesitated, flashing a silent prayer upward for wisdom.

"I'd be honored to," he replied. "However," Theodor continued delicately, "according to the Bible, pork is an unclean food. I can't really ask God's blessing over it."

The family stared at him. The host looked at the hostess for a moment, she nodded and then quickly whisked the meat from the table.

"Go ahead," the host said. "Can you offer the blessing now?"

"I'd be glad to," said Theodor.

"So why do you believe that some foods are unclean?" they asked him after lunch. "Weren't the Bible health laws given to the Jews at Sinai, and didn't they end when Jesus died?"

"Those health principles were given long before the Jews," Theodor said, wishing his father were present to explain it better.

"Noah knew about them, for there were two of every unclean animal, and seven of every clean on the ark. In fact, the Bible talks about unclean creatures even when referencing the end of the world."*

"But the New Testament talks about all things being clean," a church member objected.

"I know the passage you're talking about," Theodor said, "but if you read the passages in context, the Bible is discussing eating ceremonially washed or unwashed foods or meat offered to idols."

"Well, God told Peter in a vision it was OK to eat unclean foods,"† said another member. "That seems pretty clear to me."

"If you look again, though," said Theodor politely, "he wasn't talking about food, but about people. Peter was never to look on any person as 'clean' or 'unclean.' "

For two hours, Theodor and the Pentecostal church members discussed what the Bible had to say about unclean foods and other topics. "The main thing," said Theodor, "is that our bodies are the temple of the Holy Spirit." The church members nodded. "The mind, body, and spirit are all connected, and one affects the other," he continued. "God gave those rules because He knows what's best for us. Our stomachs and digestive systems are no different from those of the Jews. Even after all this time, His guidelines for healthful living still count."

It was now time for the afternoon meeting. Theodor said a quiet prayer for his father's sermon. He always enjoyed hearing Onofre preach.

Onofre had taken careful mental note of the texts that were used in the morning sermon. At the afternoon meeting, he used those same texts again, explaining them in the light of other scriptures. Onofre's explanations and thoughts were new for the congregation, and all listened with rapt attention. Following the afternoon sermon,

---

* See Genesis 7:1, 2; Revelation 18:2.
† See Acts 10:9–23.

the church members asked many questions, and, again, Theodor and Onofre led out in a lengthy discussion.

Glancing at the clock and then out the window at the sun hanging low in the west, Theodor knew it would soon be time to get back to camp, but the discussion seemed nowhere near ending. Eventually, the sun began to set.

"We've got to get back to our station," Onofre told the grateful congregation. After warm farewells, Onofre and Theodor set out for their camp, thankful for the fellowship with other Christians and hopeful that their discussions would prompt further Bible study.

While walking back through a stretch of lonely road between the village and their camp, a man with a gun suddenly confronted the pair.

"Show me your identification cards," he demanded. Theodor began to reach for his pocket. "Keep your hands out of your pocket!" he yelled. Theodor froze and took his hands back. The man then reached into Theodor's pocket and then into Onofre's, fishing out the papers. The gunman stared at the German IDs for a moment and then shoved the papers back. "Get out of here," he said. Theodor and his father obeyed.

"Who was he?" Theodor asked Onofre. "He didn't even tell us what he wanted."

"I don't know," replied Onofre. "But the sooner we get out of this territory, the better. I'm anxious to know how your mother and the children are doing."

"Me too," Theodor said. "But I'm still hoping the Soviets won't take over west Ukraine and we can return home."

"Yes," agreed his father. "So much depends on which way the war is going. You don't suppose the Germans are actually losing the war on the eastern front?"

"Our leaders definitely don't believe that," interjected Theodor. "Why else have they kept us lingering at each stop along our journey?"

"You're right," Onofre replied. "Every time we listen to the news, the only things we hear about are the German victories. It's hard to believe the rumors that they are losing, yet the signs are everywhere. As for me, I'm tired of waiting. I wish the radio could give us accurate information."

"When have they ever?" Theodor complained. "Misinformation, that's always been the way with the Third Reich. If only we could find out for sure what's happening." He kicked a stone on the road. "All this sitting around and waiting is driving me crazy."

"Me too," his father said. "But God is not wasting the time. Just look at the day we've had. God always has His own timing." Theodor nodded.

Back at the camp, Theodor and another man from the group, Stephan, discussed the wait again. Suddenly, Theodor had an idea.

"Let's take the train and go back as far as the railroad goes," Theodor suggested. "From there we can go on by foot to the eastern front. Then we can see for ourselves how the war is going and bring back the news to everyone here."

"Sounds great," Stephan agreed. "And while we're at it, I'd be interested in making a bit of money. We could do a little business back there near the war zone."

"What do you mean?" Theodor asked.

"When the Russians take over, the German currency will lose all its value," he answered. "The Ukrainians back there know it, and they'll want to get something for their German money before it becomes completely worthless."

Theodor's eyes brightened. "But for us, this far away, and then in Germany, the money will still be good!" Theodor exclaimed. "What an excellent plan. What can we sell?"

"How about matches and flint stone?" Stephan suggested. "Everyone needs those items, and I'm sure they're in short supply back there."

"Let's do it," cried Theodor, eager to be off and doing something.

"I'm not sure that's such a good idea," Onofre said when Theodor revealed his plan. "We've come a long way already. I'd hate to see you stuck in the war zone—or worse. There are always air raids, and, besides, your German citizenship won't get you out of trouble forever."

"Don't worry about me," said Theodor. "With no one to slow us down, Stephan and I will be gone and back before you know it. And we'll bring back extra cash to help the family out. It ought to come in handy when we make it to Germany."

"You make your own decisions now," Onofre said reluctantly. "Come back soon."

The next morning, Theodor and his companion bought a large supply of matches and flint, setting out with grand expectations. They boarded the train and settled in for the long journey back over the countryside their company had just labored for months to cover. One night the Russians began bombing a train station where the travelers were stopped, waiting for a transfer. Many tall buildings towered above the station, and heavy debris rained down from the explosions. *Maybe this trip wasn't such a good idea,* Theodor thought, scrambling under a bench. *But we've come too far to turn back now.*

The train finally arrived at the last railroad station, and the conductor announced that the train could go no farther into the war zone. Theodor and Stephan resumed their journey toward the front lines on foot. They passed throngs of refugees on the roads, headed the opposite direction. While walking, they occasionally saw a large German military motorcycle roaring past, the leader of another refugee group.

"The Germans assigned a special military troubleshooter for all us refugees," someone told Theodor. "He goes back and forth between us and the front lines to tell us when the Russian troops are beginning to advance."

"Just like our SS-Oberscharführer did," Theodor said. "Can the troubleshooter tell us about the war itself?" Theodor said.

"Don't bother," another refugee said. "We've all tried to get that information, but he never informs us about the war itself. We just have to move when it's time to move."

"Sounds familiar," said Theodor to Stephan. "I guess we'll have to keep on going and see for ourselves."

After selling all their matches and flint to the local Ukrainians and making a good profit, the two set out for the hills where they had been told the front line was supposed to be. Scrambling through the bushes, they listened for gunfire in the distance, but the only thing they heard was their own rustling and an occasional cry from a lonely bird. This was where the war was supposed to be, but it seemed abnormally quiet.

"Where's the fighting?" Theodor whispered to his friend. "Are we in the right place?"

"I don't know," Stephan replied. "Let's keep on going until we see some action."

All at once a German officer popped up seemingly from nowhere. His eyes sized them up, two scraggly Ukrainians poking around in a war zone.

"Follow me," the rough man ordered. Theodor and Stephan obeyed. The officer walked ahead of them in silence. After a while, he stopped, pulled out a handgun out of his pouch and started to reload it. This wasn't the kind of action Theodor had wanted to see. The foolishness of what he and Stephan were doing struck him at the same time as the realization of what the officer intended to do. He stared at the handgun in horror.

All the money they could make, all the news they could bring back from the front didn't matter anymore.

"Start talking," whispered Theodor to his friend in Ukrainian. "Or this is all the action we'll ever see again."

Chapter 9

Theodor and Stephan stared at their executioner. Could this really be happening?

"Sir," protested Theodor's older friend. "Wait. We are German citizens, and we just wanted to see our homes again."

Theodor prayed silently.

Surprised to hear German from two Ukrainians, the officer stopped loading and looked up. He frowned skeptically.

"Let me see your ID cards," he demanded. The two hastily pulled the papers out of their coat pockets. The officer scrutinized the IDs suspiciously, before handing the passports back. Shaking his head, he muttered under his breath. "Stupid, stupid."

"Get out of this area at once," he ordered curtly, replacing the gun in its holster. Then he headed off away from them.

Thank You, Lord, for not giving up on me, even though I made the foolish choice to come back, Theodor prayed quietly.

"What are we doing here?" Stephan said. "This was a stupid idea. I thought for sure we were goners."

"Me too," said Theodor. "Let's see how fast we can get back." Losing all interest in the war or in making more money, they raced back to the train depot.

Though their journey had taken them nearly three weeks to

come that far, Theodor and Stephan lost no time in retracing their path to the rest of their group. In their haste, it took only a couple days to return.

Back at the camp, they reported the little news they had learned. Germany was indeed losing. "There is no point in waiting any longer," Theodor told the refugees. "Forget about going back home."

"The closer we get to the German border, the safer we will be," said Stephan. The whole company agreed. After this, the refugees moved steadily on, staying in any one place for only one night before moving on again.

One evening as the group was getting ready to retire for a short night's rest, a Ukrainian man approached. He singled out Theodor, who was grooming his horse at the edge of the camp.

"Hey, you," the man called to Theodor in Ukrainian. Theodor raised his head.

Me? Why did he approach me? wondered Theodor, looking around at the others. There were many older men in the group with whom the stranger could chat.

"Where are you heading to?" the man demanded.

"Germany," Theodor replied.

"Why?" he asked, drawing closer. "Aren't you Ukrainian?"

"I was born Ukrainian," Theodor answered. "I'm a German citizen now."

"Well," the stranger said, "The Ukrainian underground movement needs young true-blooded Ukrainians like you. We cannot let you go to Germany."

"What!" exclaimed Theodor. "No, that is out of the question."

"You must stay with us and serve our country," the man insisted. "Your country needs you."

"I have my father with me," argued Theodor. "He is getting old, and he needs me too."

"We will come back later and talk with your father," the man replied forebodingly. He then sauntered off toward the forest.

We? thought Theodor. He looked up and saw the shadows of other men—Ukrainian guerilla soldiers—lurking in the shadows of the trees.

Theodor quickly reported this information to his group.

"They will indeed come back," said the SS-Oberscharführer, grimacing, "but they're not going to have a talk with your father. They'll be back tonight to kidnap you."

"Kidnap me!" Theodor raged at the thought. "They wouldn't dare."

"Just watch," the leader warned. "We'll have to be on full alert throughout the night."

Over me? Theodor wondered. He thought about the beating that the führer had given him. Ever since that day, the SS-Oberscharführer had left him alone; Theodor made it a point to act as if the incident had never happened. *Why would he care to save me from being kidnapped?* Theodor wondered. *I'm surprised.*

Throughout the night, each of the men stood guard with rifles and hand grenades at the ready, waiting for the attack to come. Eventually, in the darkest hours of early morning, the vigilant group of refugees saw the would-be-kidnappers circling the camp, looking for a way in to grab Theodor. But the defense strategy held. As morning dawned, the Ukrainian guerrillas slunk away.

"God has a different plan for your life than what they have in mind for you, Theodor," Onofre reminded him. "Never forget that." Theodor nodded, reflecting how God had repeatedly spared his life and, in this case, his freedom.

Early in the morning, the tired group of refugees continued their journey. Arriving at the border a few days later, they crossed into what became East Germany. Reaching the city of Ratibor, the men received orders from the SS-Oberscharführer to hitch their horses and wagons on one side of the street and to line up one last time. Theodor watched as the SS-Oberscharführer started down the line, shaking each man's hand, bidding each one a final farewell.

I don't know what to say to him, thought Theodor, remembering the beating. *I suppose nothing.*

When the SS-Oberscharführer extended his hand to Theodor, the gruff man broke into tears. Throwing his arms around Theodor, he hugged him, weeping on Theodor's shoulder. The officer would hardly let him go. Theodor awkwardly hugged the man back. He was surprised and touched. *I guess he's telling me he's sorry,* Theodor reasoned, trying to make sense of it.

"Goodbye," Theodor told the officer warmly. "Thank you for your leadership."

"Heil Hitler," the officer finally managed, collecting his emotions. Theodor returned the salute. *I hope he survives the war,* Theodor thought, watching the man move down the line. *God has a plan for his life too. I hope he finds it.*

In Ratibor, German officials took away the refugees' personal horses and wagons. The weapons also were confiscated.

"You won't need these anymore," the Germans told them. The refugees packed the leftover artillery and ammunition from their stash onto a freight train headed back to the war zone. Theodor felt no remorse at seeing the weapons go.

"Before you leave to your final destination, you all are invited to a big meal sponsored by the German government," the SS-Oberscharführer said. "Welcome to Germany!"

After subsisting on little more than dried bread for months, the invitation thrilled Theodor. But when they sat down to the dinner, his hopes for a feast fizzled when he saw the main dish was once again pork. Remaining true to conscience, Theodor and Onofre ate only the side dishes offered, leaving the main course for their hungry companions.

After eating and visiting with their fellow refugees and the German authorities, Theodor and his father boarded a train bound for Mährisch Trübau, Sudetenland.* Onofre and Theodor hoped they would be reunited there with the rest of their family. The train journey from Ratibor to Mährisch Trübau took two days.

---

* At the time, this region was under Germany's control. After the war, it belonged to Poland again.

Each freight car carried several families, along with their belongings.

At one stop, a new family boarded their car. As the miles of rail clacked by, Theodor gradually took greater notice of the new family. They looked like any other refugee family, but there was something about their behavior—they didn't smoke or curse, their clothing was simple, and they were kind to everybody. For some reason, the family kept staring in his and his father's direction, especially when Theodor and his father tried to read their Bibles by the faint light coming through the slats in the freight car.

"Why do they keep staring at us?" Theodor whispered to his father.

"I don't know," Onofre answered. "Why don't you go ask them?"

"That's OK," said Theodor. "If they want to talk with us, they'll come over."

On the following day, the family could resist no longer. Theodor looked up to see them picking their way over to the corner he shared with this father.

"Hello," said Onofre, smiling.

"Excuse us," the man of the family replied. "Are you by any chance Seventh-day Adventists?"

"Yes!" said Theodor.

"So are we," they exclaimed, beaming with delight.

Theodor and his father invited the family to share the rest of the trip with them. What a pleasure it was for both families to travel together. Along with a shared lifestyle, they also shared the same understanding of the future and a concern for the present time.

"My biggest worry concerns our employment in this new place," said Onofre. "I worked for myself as a weaver in the Ukraine and could observe the Sabbath without worrying about a boss. Taking the Sabbath off may not be so easy now that we are in Germany." In 1944, there were not many Seventh-day Adventists in Europe.

"We are concerned too," said the other Adventist man. "Not many people know us, and I suspect that getting the Sabbath off will be difficult."

"Especially in Germany," added Theodor, "where the Jewish stigma attached to the Sabbath is so strong."

"I know that God will take care of us, come what may," said Onofre, always the man of faith. "It has never been a matter of convenience." Theodor always gained courage from his father's strength and steady convictions. For Onofre, it did not matter if the whole world was against them, as long as they were following God's will.

* — * — * — *

In May, after a four-month journey, Theodor and his father rejoiced in reuniting with the rest of their family. Back together at last, everyone had many stories to share.

The hair on Theodor's arms and neck stood up as he listened to his mother's harrowing tale.

Caroline told how the train loaded with all the mothers and children had arrived in one of the Polish cities. It was late in the evening. The station where they had to disembark from the train lay somewhat outside the city. The travelers would board another train continuing their journey in the morning, but for now they had to walk from the station into the city, where the German authorities had prepared a place for them to stay overnight.

All the mothers and their children left the train station together, following a guide toward the designated place. But with five children in tow, ages two to sixteen years old, Caroline could not keep pace with the rest of the group. As darkness closed around them, Caroline's family fell farther and farther behind.* Caroline plodded on in the general direction of the city, but with no lights permitted due the threat of enemy air raids, she soon grew disoriented, unsure of the route.

---

* Caroline had six children with her: Slawko was 18, Daria was 16, Theophil was 11, Vladimir was 8, Enoch was 4, and Thomas was 2. Slawko did not stay much with the family. Throughout the journey, Slawko kept company with the boys his own age, while the other children stayed with their mother all the time. During this incident, Slawko had gone on ahead.

Encountering a Polish man, apparently headed the same direction, Caroline asked, "Have you seen a large group of women and children going to town?"

"Yes," he said. "If you follow me, I will take you there."

Relieved, Caroline followed the man. At the train station, the women had been told that it was not far to the lodging place, but after following the stranger for a while, they seemed no closer to their destination. Caroline noticed that the streets were getting narrower and narrower. There were no houses anymore, and it did not appear as though they were getting near the city at all. It was almost midnight, and the children were exhausted. "I'm hungry. I'm thirsty," they complained. "Are we almost there?"

"I'm turning back," Caroline said to the Polish man. "My children cannot walk any longer."

"No, no. We're almost there," the man insisted.

After a short while they came to a bridge, a river splashing in the darkness far below. Caroline then realized, with a start, that they were in the middle of nowhere.

"Where have you brought us?" Caroline challenged.

"To die," the man said. "I hate Ukrainians."

"Wait," Caroline cried. "We're German citizens!"

"All this time I have heard you and your children speaking in Ukrainian," the man replied, unbending. "I hate Ukrainians." The man pulled out his gun. "I'm going to kill you all right here and throw you into the river."

Terrified, Caroline and her children tried to fight back, but the man was too strong for them. They were staring in the face of death. *He's possessed with demons,* thought Caroline. Alone in this desolate place, no one would ever know their fate. Caroline knew only divine help would spare their lives from this maniac.

"Give me just a little time for prayer with my children," she begged.

"Go ahead," the man agreed. He had no reason to hurry, there was nowhere for the family to escape.

Caroline huddled with her children, and, in the language the man hated and couldn't understand, she prayed that the Lord would not let this evil man go any further with his brutal design. It was midnight; no one was around for miles, when, suddenly, the headlights of a large truck beamed over the bridge, the roar of its engine breaking the stillness. Too relieved to wonder where it had come from, Caroline and the children raised their hands.

"Help!" they cried, frantically waving their arms. The truck screeched to a stop beside them. The murderer leaped away into the darkness and was gone.

The truck driver and his passenger, helpful and sympathetic, piled the frightened family into the back of the truck. Caroline and the children huddled together to keep warm as the driver headed back to the city. After finding the lodging place and dropping them off with the rest of their group, the truck quickly left. The rest of the mothers were horrified to hear their story. Word soon was carried to the German authorities in charge of the trip. "We wish we could get a hold of this maniac before he kills somebody" was all the German officials could say.

Caroline, her children, and the rest of the refugee families with her were sent on to Mährisch Trübau. There they were assigned barracks on the outskirts of the city. The large wooden structures had no insulation, but they were adequate and a welcome refuge after the frightening trip.

"God has repeatedly spared our lives through this journey," Onofre said, hugging his family close and leading them in praises, thanking God for the divine protection during their months of separation.

* — * — * — *

Theodor spent a few days acquainting himself with the new environment in Mährisch Trübau. His family had always lived on a farm. Living in town was a significant change for all of them. Everything seemed cramped together, including the barracks and bunk beds on which the family slept. At home in the Ukraine, the Paw-luks owned a large house with plenty of room for all. There they had grown most of their own food, harvesting fresh produce. Now Caroline depended on food stamps for their meager food supply. At home the family had spoken in Ukrainian and Russian; here they had to talk in German. Even the social greetings were different: "Good morning," "Good day," and "Good evening" were all replaced with "Heil Hitler."

We lost and risked so much just to get away from the Communists, Theodor reflected to himself. *But how much have we actually gained? There seems to be little difference between Communism and Nazism. The suffering is the same.*

A few days after reuniting with their family, Theodor and his father received a notice in the mail from the *Arbeitsamt,* the German "employment office," that they must both report to work at the *Metalbau,* a local "defense plant." Their jobs there were to repair the damaged airplanes that had returned from combat missions. Theodor found it an interesting job, and, for the most part, he enjoyed working at the factory, learning new skills.

Sometimes, Theodor momentarily forgot he was in Germany. Passing by his boss one day, Theodor greeted him with a chipper "Good morning."

"Pardon me?" the boss said icily, stopping Theodor.

"Heil Hitler," Theodor said, chagrined.

"That's much better," the boss snapped, walking past. Theodor pursed his lips. *When in Rome, do as the Romans do,* thought Theodor, vowing to be more careful.

Even in the middle of the working day, Germany was never safe from the Allies' air raids. Every day the city endured at least one, if not more, air attacks. When the siren wailed its warning signal, all the workers ran into the basement for protection, not knowing whether they would come out alive. At Theodor's plant, the basements were just storage rooms and not designed to serve as bunkers for air attacks. The daily bombardments continued for more than a year.

Theodor was thankful that the *Metalbau* was not on the Allies' maps. Other factories in the city were not so lucky. When they were bombed, hundreds of workers were killed. Theodor and his father were told that the phosphorus bombs were the most dangerous ones. Not only did the bombs destroy the buildings, but when they fell on the street, the asphalt melted. Even though the danger was so great, the workers were still required to come to work every day.

Theodor and Onofre carried out their assignments in the *Metalbau* faithfully. Except on Saturdays. On the Sabbath, they both stayed home.

After more than a month of this, the foreman approached Theodor. "You must not miss work on Saturday morning anymore," he told Theodor.

"It's my Sabbath," explained Theodor. "I cannot come into work—for religious reasons."

The foreman frowned. "But that's Jewish."

"No," said Theodor. "The Jews are not the only ones who worship on Saturday."

"Well, I expect to see you here next Saturday," said the foreman, ending the discussion.

"Did the foreman talk to you, too, about Saturday?" Theodor asked his father.

"Not a word to me," said Onofre. "We've been blessed to be able to escape notice for such a long time."

"I would think the foreman would have said something to you also if he had really been serious," reasoned Theodor.

"Would it make any difference to you?" asked Onofre.

"No," said Theodor. "You know I still wouldn't work."

Theodor and Onofre again missed work on Saturday morning as usual. Breaking the Sabbath just wasn't an option.

Sunday morning there was a knock at the Pawluks' barracks. Caroline opened the door to two German policemen.

"We'd like to see Onofre and Theodor Pawluk," the officers said.

Theodor and his father came to the door. Caroline and the rest of the children gathered nearby to listen.

"I am Onofre. Can we help you?" asked Onofre.

"You and Theodor are under arrest," one officer announced. Caroline gasped. After a moment of shock, the tears began. The family had forsaken their homeland, coming to Germany to avoid Communist oppression, and here, only a few weeks after their arrival, Theodor and Onofre were headed to prison.

"Both of you, follow us to the police station," the officer ordered, motioning to Onofre and Theodor. The policemen had no car, only bicycles.

"If you behave yourselves and do not try to escape from us, we will not handcuff you," they told Theodor and Onofre.

"Don't worry," responded Onofre. "We are Christians. We will not try to escape."

The officers just grunted. "Because you are under arrest, you have also lost your citizens' rights," one said. "You are not permitted to walk on the sidewalk."

Saying a tearful goodbye to the family, Theodor and Onofre followed after the policemen, walking in the street. It was to the officers' advantage not to handcuff their prisoners since the policemen were riding their bicycles. Theodor and his father walked quickly, trying to keep up.

During the one-kilometer trek to the police station, Onofre struck up a conversation with one of the policemen. Onofre had noticed that the German uniform had belt buckles engraved with the slogan *Gott Mit Uns,* "God with us."

"Do you believe what's written on your buckles?" Onofre asked the police officer who was a little ahead of him on the bike. The Nazi cursed God's name. Theodor cringed to hear the foul language directed at God. It was even worse than anything he had heard the Communists say.

"If I were you, I would be afraid to talk about God like that," Onofre warned. But the officer did so even more. *Talking to the of-*

ficer about God is like casting pearls before swine, thought Theodor.

At the station, the police checked their names and address, following the routine procedure with the prisoners.

"Lock them up," an officer told one of the guards. Theodor and Onofre followed the man down a long corridor, their footsteps echoing down the hall.

"Here you are," the guard announced, opening a thick iron door into a small jail cell. "Give me your belts and shoestrings." He waited with open hand. Puzzled, Theodor looked at the guard as he started undoing his laces. "So you don't hang yourselves," the guard explained tersely. "Here's a bucket for your physical needs." After handing over the bucket, the guard locked them in the cell, and Theodor could hear his footsteps echoing back down the hallway. Theodor and Onofre were alone for the rest of the day.

The small cell was empty—no bed, no sink, no table, no bench, just four walls and a floor. The two stood for a while, then sat down on the floor, their backs against the wall, waiting for the worst.

Onofre and Theodor had no hearing, no attorney, no court procedure. No one told them why they were arrested or how long they would be kept in jail. They had no idea what the police might do to them. They just sat on the floor and talked and prayed. In the evening, the warden gave them a small meal—one slice of bread and lukewarm water to drink. After the meal Theodor and Onofre sat down again on the floor and talked some more, wondering what the future held. Eventually, as weariness caught up with them, the two prisoners lay down on the hard floor and fell asleep.

Early the next morning, the lights turned on. Waking up, Theodor realized that they were not home but in prison. *What will happen next?* Theodor wondered grimly. Soon a small window opened and the warden pushed breakfast through. Another small slice of bread for each of them and a cup of water. A few minutes later an officer brought back their belts and shoestrings.

"Get ready to go," the officer said, waiting outside the cell while Onofre and Theodor finished dressing.

Where are they taking us? Theodor wondered, threading his belt through his loose pants. *To a bigger prison or to the concentration camp where they burn the prisoners alive? Maybe even to a quick execution.* The possibilities depressed Theodor, but there was no way out. For a moment he wished he had some water with which to wash and shave and a change of clothing. Then reality hit him. *Who cares?* he asked himself. *Grooming doesn't matter now.* A barrage of imagined horrors filled his mind. *So this is the way it's going to end,* he thought bleakly.

"Follow me," the officer said, leading the way out of the cell. He didn't bother to handcuff them.

"Where are we going?" Theodor asked.

"No talking!" the policeman yelled in German. "Especially not in Ukrainian." Theodor's heart hammered in his chest. As his father followed the officer out the door, Theodor trailed behind. Walking the long hall, early in the morning, with no one else around, the only thing Theodor heard was the officer's heavy boots hitting the hard floor and their own softer footsteps. *It's our death march,* Theodor brooded.

The three of them were alone in the corridor, Theodor at the end of it, when suddenly, Theodor felt a tapping on his left shoulder.

Startled, his eyes widened. The only sounds of footsteps came from in front of him. But he hadn't imagined the touch. Afraid to stop, Theodor turned his head to look.

Chapter 10

In the early morning light, Theodor turned to see the most kind and peaceful face he had ever seen looking straight into his eyes.

"Don't be afraid," a gentle voice said. "The Lord will be with you." Theodor, still not breaking pace, and now electrified with this second shock, stared at the speaker's smiling eyes.

"Where are they taking us?" Theodor was about to blurt, when the face vanished from beside him.

Such peace as Theodor had never felt before overflowed within him. Joy filled his heart. It did not matter where the police took them now. God was truly with Theodor and Onofre, His angels watching over their every step. The supernatural visit flooded Theodor with fresh courage, and a familiar chorus came to his mind.

> Turn your eyes upon Jesus,
> Look full in His wonderful face;
> And the things of earth will grow strangely dim
> In the light of His glory and grace.

Theodor nearly sang the words out loud. He wanted to tell his father, still trudging ahead of him behind their prison escort, but he knew he must keep silent. No talking was permitted. In silence they walked out of the prison and down to the railroad depot a half hour's walking distance away. There they boarded the train. Because the Nazi regime controlled everything in the system, including the railroad, they did not need any tickets to board the train. The railway car was empty when they first arrived. The officer selected a place where all three of them could sit together, where he could keep watch over the prisoners.

As the other passengers began boarding the train and the car was nearly full, a young woman who knew Theodor entered the car. Her face brightened to see Theodor, and, having no idea that he and his father were under arrest, she immediately made her way toward him.

"Hi, Theo," she exclaimed. "Where are you going?"

"You cannot talk to him!" the policeman impulsively shouted at her. "He is under arrest." Startled, she stopped and stared at him, then at Theodor. He smiled sheepishly back at her. All the other passengers began staring also. The officer shifted on the seat, upset that he had blown his cover.

"Oh," said Theodor's acquaintance, sitting down silently into a nearby seat. Theodor now felt every passenger in the car looking at him and his father. From the looks on their faces, they couldn't see anything wrong with the two arrestees—they weren't even in handcuffs. The train began to lurch down the track. As the wheels settled into a rhythm, the people around Onofre and Theodor continued to stare and whisper, sometimes shaking their heads sympathetically. Theodor sensed their pity. So did the officer. An hour passed.

"These two men are Seventh-day Adventists," the officer, fed up with the glances, finally announced to the passengers. "They refuse to work on Saturday because it is their Sabbath," he spit out. "If everybody were like them, the Russians could come and take us over at any time."

Theodor had only suspected the cause of their arrest, but now he knew for sure.

A few hours later the train arrived in Zwickau, where there was a large prison. Here, the policeman turned Theodor and Onofre over to the prison authorities.

"How did they behave on the train?" a prison guard asked, frowning. He eyed the uncuffed hands of the prisoners.

"They were OK," the police officer answered.

In the prison, the guards took away Theodor and his father's clothing, replacing it with prison outfits that had large black numbers emblazoned on their backs. The guards put the pair together in a cell with other inmates. Inside the cell, communication was forbidden. When hearing any talking or commotion, the prison guards would burst in and brutally beat the offenders. Zwickau Prison had no exercise area and no literature to read. No talking of any kind was permitted among the inmates. All the prisoners could do was to sit quietly in the prison cell and wait—for what, no one knew.

Every so often a Gestapo officer would open the door and call out a prisoner's name. A prisoner so summoned was seldom brought back. These prisoners were usually beaten, if not to death, then nearly so and placed in the hospital. From there, most mysteriously disappeared. Only a few were lucky enough to return to prison.

Sometimes, on a good day, the guards would take trustworthy prisoners to load or to unload the train or to clean the city parks. For Theodor and his father, these outdoor assignments provided a welcome change of pace and the occasional chance to talk. It was on one of these occasions that Theodor was finally able to share the angel's message with his father.

One day, a Gestapo officer took just the two of them, Onofre and Theodor, to clean up the city plaza, the park in the center of town. They swept the sidewalks, scrubbed pigeon droppings off benches, raked the grass, picked up trash, and fished out debris from the small fountain. They worked quickly, finishing the job in just a few hours.

"What else can we do, sir?" Theodor asked. The Gestapo officer frowned while he surveyed the tidy park, looking in vain for something to criticize.

The city plaza, a central gathering place for old and young alike, was never empty. Youth around Theodor's age hung out by the fountain; young women strolled on the sidewalks and flirted with the young men. Old men sat on park benches enjoying the shade, while little children frolicked on the grass beneath the trees.

The officer grunted. "Take your rakes and put them on your shoulders," he commanded. Theodor and Onofre swung their rakes up, both looking at their boss quizzically. "Now march," he ordered.

"Where, sir?" Onofre asked.

"Straight ahead, through the park. Now one, two, three, four. One, two, three, four." Theodor and his father obeyed their new drill sergeant, puzzled as to why the man would show appreciation for their good work by debasing them. "Pick up your feet," the officer barked. "Higher! Right face, march. One, two, three, four. Left face, march."

A flock of teenaged girls twittered as Theodor, his father behind him, marched by under the orders of their commander-in-chief. Theodor's face burned with embarrassment. As he passed his peers at the fountain, the young men clapped their hands at the performance. The old men chuckled with amusement at the display. Back and forth, back and forth, the prisoners marched under the green trees. The Gestapo man scoffed at his prisoners, calling out insulting names.

Theodor wanted to throw his rake down and leave, but he kept his eyes straight ahead and obeyed the mocking orders behind him. At the age of nineteen, he wanted to look good and be welcomed into society. It was hard for him to be so despised and ridiculed in front of all the people. Theodor seethed and gritted his teeth.

Then a picture of Jesus plodding down the road to Calvary appeared in his mind. As he thought of how his Lord was ridiculed, despised, and rejected, then nailed to the cross to die, Theodor realized that what he was going through for Him was nothing compared to Christ's suffering and death for him. *Thank You, Lord,* Theodor prayed quietly. He ignored the stares and tried to focus on the beautiful day outside the prison walls.

————*——*

One day in the prison, after a skimpy breakfast, the door of their section clanged open and another uniformed Gestapo officer entered the cell.

"Theodor Pawluk," he announced. An undercurrent of sympathy rippled among the other prisoners. Theodor saw his father tense. When a lone prisoner was called out, it was never good. Theodor cast a glance of love and farewell to his father. Onofre nodded at him. Theodor stood up, his stomach in knots, his knees unsteady. The officer motioned for Theodor to follow him.

Why did they call me and not my father? Theodor wondered. *Surely my father would be able to answer questions more thoroughly than I can. But I am younger and stronger than my father now. It's better this way.* Theodor took a deep breath and, again, tried not to think of what awaited him.

He followed the Gestapo officer up to the interrogation-room door.

"Open this door and step in," the man instructed. He left Theodor there, gulping at the door. Praying for courage, Theodor turned the door knob. A moan of pain assaulted his ears. Stepping inside the room, Theodor flinched at what he saw.

An interrogator, with a mustache as thick as his scowl, stood behind a large desk, his arms crossed, watching as two Gestapo officers clubbed a bloody body curled up on the floor. Theodor moved into a corner of the room and stood there like a piece of petrified wood awaiting his own sentence. Once in a while the Gestapo officer shot him a dirty look. "You're next," the look told him.

After the officers had finished beating the prisoner with their clubs, they handed the injured man a bucket of water and a rag, forcing him to wash off his own blood from the walls, the floor, and the office furniture. To make sure that he did not miss anything, all three officers meticulously searched for any drops of blood, pointing them out, until the prisoner was finished.

When the prisoner finished wiping his blood from the office, paramedics came in with a stretcher and carried him away. The two Gestapo officers then put their clubs in their belts and left the room also, one of them flicking a foreboding smile at Theodor. Now the interrogator and Theodor were alone in the room. The interrogator straightened the chairs and the papers on his desk and then sat down behind it.

"Sit down," the interrogator invited, motioning Theodor to sit opposite him at the desk. The interrogator tilted his chin and sized up Theodor, narrowing his eyes in scrutiny. The man leaned back in his chair and tapped his fingers together.

"Why do you refuse to work on Saturday?" he asked straight out. Theodor took a deep breath. Just as he suspected.

" 'Remember the Sabbath day to keep it holy,' " Theodor started quoting the fourth commandment. " 'Six days shalt thou labour, and do all thy work: But the seventh day is the Sabbath of the Lord thy God: In it thou shalt not do any work, thou, nor thy . . .' "*

"That is all Jewish!" the interrogator shouted. "Jewish," he pounded the table again.

Great, thought Theodor. *The last thing I need right now is to be identified with the Jews.* He cast a quick glance at the corner of the interrogator's desk. A black call button waited for a simple push from the questioner to bring the Gestapo bursting back in. If Theodor didn't cooperate, he, too, would soon be mopping up his own blood.

---

* Exodus 20:8–10.

"But Adam and Eve were not Jews," Theodor said kindly, "yet they observed the Sabbath."

"Saturday is not the seventh day as you said it was," the interrogator nearly shouted, ignoring Theodor's reply.

"According to the calendar it is," said Theodor very softly, hoping to de-escalate the man's anger.

The interrogator cast a haughty look at Theodor as he took the calendar down from the wall behind him.

"All right, show me," he challenged, slapping the calendar down on the desk in front of him. Theodor got up and stretched himself across the desk to look.

"See how the weeks are divided by the thick black line," Theodor pointed out gently. Then he started to read below the line in German.

"Eins, zwei, drei, vier, fünf, sechs, sieben." Theodor rested his finger on the last day, Saturday. For a long moment the interrogator said nothing. Theodor resisted the urge to say more.

What will happen now? Will he call back the Gestapo? Theodor sent a silent prayer heavenward.

The man finally looked at Theodor, a dazed look on his face. *"Menschenskind, das wusste ich nicht."* "For goodness' sake, I did not know that." Godly fear must have seized him, for quickly his demeanor changed.

"We must get you out of here before they change you to ashes," the interrogator said, his voice low. He looked up quickly at the door as if he did not want to be caught by the Gestapo talking to a prisoner like that. This was an interrogation after all, not a Bible study.

"So," he said, clearing his throat and changing the subject. "What is your occupation, besides what you are doing now?"

"Tailoring," Theodor said.

"Would you do some tailoring for me and my family?" he asked.

"I would be glad to," Theodor answered. "I enjoy tailoring very much."

The man grunted in reply, made a few notes on a form in front of him, and reached for the black button. Theodor held his breath.

The two Gestapo officers walked back into the room.

"Take the prisoner back to his cell," the interrogator commanded one of the men. Theodor exhaled with relief. The officer looked disappointed, but he escorted Theodor back to his cell without comment. Theodor kept his eyes on the floor as he passed another prisoner waiting to be called in for interrogation. As Theodor entered his familiar cell, the other prisoners looked up in shock to see him back so soon. His father beamed to see him, but with no speaking allowed, Theodor could only smile at Onofre, trying to reassure him that everything was OK.

The next morning the guard came back and called Theodor again. This time, the guard led him up a long flight of stairs to the interrogator's apartment on the top floor of the prison complex.

Tailoring for the interrogator's family was a pleasant respite from prison life. For the first time in a long time, Theodor received three good meals a day. He played with the family's children and almost felt as if he were home. He altered and repaired the interrogator's clothing as needed, as well as the clothing of the man's wife and children.

Theodor sensed that this was not an acceptable time to talk about his faith, but he could live it. Every stitch he sewed, every buttonhole he made, and every button he sewed on, he made it the best way he knew how. "Let your light so shine before men, that they may see your good works, and glorify your Father which is in heaven," Theodor remembered.* After nearly two weeks, he finished mending the last article of clothing, and the interrogator sent Theodor back to his prison cell.

When his father looked up to see his son standing there, healthy, strong, and happy, he nearly fainted with surprise. Onofre still

---

* Matthew 5:16.

knew nothing of the interrogation, nor of the tailoring, so he had assumed the worst. Overjoyed, he couldn't stop smiling. Theodor still couldn't explain what had happened, but from his health and vigor, Onofre knew his prayers for his son's safety had been answered.

One day, not long after Theodor had returned, a guard took Theodor, his father, and a few others to the railroad station to unload an incoming freight train. Even though it was hard work, Theodor and Onofre enjoyed it far better than sitting all day in the prison cell. The two still didn't have the opportunity to talk though.

It was now September 1944—the potato harvesting season.

"I urgently need help harvesting my potato crop before the rains begin," a farmer near Zwickau told the prison officials one day. "Can you send any prisoners to assist me?" he inquired.

Without delay, the prison guards took Theodor, Onofre, and some other prisoners out to the farm to dig up the potatoes. The prisoners were divided into teams of two. Each team was assigned a basket to fill. Theodor rejoiced when the guards appointed his father as his partner.

Theodor always enjoyed working with Onofre, but now this time together was especially precious. At last, with the guards standing far enough away to give them a little privacy, they could talk.

Speaking in quiet, guarded tones, Theodor told his father all about the interrogation and about the two wonderful weeks Theodor had spent tailoring. Onofre's eyes brimmed with tears.

"The Lord has indeed been with you, Theo," he said, remembering the angel's message to his son. "After you told me about that special visit, I knew that everything would be OK. It gave me such hope, especially when you were taken away for those two weeks. But I never knew if I would see you again." Onofre threw a potato into the basket.

"I knew you were praying for me," said Theodor, digging in the soil for another. "And I remembered the promise that 'all things work together for good to them that love God, to them who are the called according to his purpose.'* I'm still trying to see how being in this prison for so long is working together for good."

"I know," Onofre said. "We may not ever understand why some things have been permitted to happen until we finally get to heaven. But even here in prison, God is working out His plans." Onofre wiped the sweat out of his eyes. The morning heat drenched the men with perspiration.

"I wish we had the answer now," Theodor said, placing a potato into the nearly full basket. "But I know you're right."

"Is it just me," Onofre mused, changing the subject, "or have you noticed that things are different in our section of the prison lately? At least I've noticed a change since you've been back after those two weeks."

"It's not just you," said Theodor. "The guards' behavior toward all the prisoners in our cell block has changed. There hasn't been harshness or yelling. And they don't beat the prisoners anymore. I wonder why." Theodor dug a potato up, shook the dirt off, and tossed it into the basket. "Let's empty this basket on the pile now." The two men lugged the large basket toward the farmer's main potato pile.

"It all began to change after your interrogation," Onofre said, panting from the heavy load. "I think it's partly because of our being here. It's our living testimony about God that may be making an impression on them."

"Jesus once said, 'Ye shall be witnesses unto me both in Jerusalem, and in all Judea, and in Samaria, and unto the uttermost part of the earth.' "† Theodor remarked, setting his end of the basket down and picking up a stray potato that had fallen from a basket emptied earlier. "I suppose that includes Zwickau Prison." As usual, father and son worked vigorously, as if it were their own farm.

---

* Romans 8:28.
† Acts 1:8.

"You're right, Theo. We are able to witness for the Lord to so many people at the prison who need Him," Onofre said, stopping to scoop up a fallen potato. " 'Be obedient to them that are your masters . . . with fear and trembling,' " he quoted again, " 'with good will doing service, as to the Lord, not to men.' "*

"The hardest part is being cheerful," Theodor replied, "but I know the Bible says to 'rejoice in the Lord, always.' "

Reciting Scripture gave them both so much comfort, especially as they weren't permitted to have a Bible in their cell. " 'In every thing give thanks: for this is the will of God in Christ Jesus concerning you.' "† Theodor added. "It's the giving thanks that is God's will, right?"

"Right. We know that misery, injustice, and death are not God's will, but in our trust and attitude, we can still give God praise. No matter what happens to us, He will have the final word, you know." They emptied the potatoes in their basket onto the heap, setting the basket back quickly as they continued digging up their row.

"I know." Theodor placed a potato into the newly emptied basket. "You always encourage me so much," he said. "I know you're worried about Mother and the kids. What do you suppose will happen to them if we don't return home?"

"I do worry about them a lot," Onofre replied. "But I'm trying to turn my worries into prayer instead. God will take care of them. Remember how He protected them on their journey to Germany? Ultimately, God is the only One they can depend on anyway. Your mother knows this, and no matter what, we will all meet again when Jesus returns."

A lump rose in Theodor's throat. He remembered how his father had lost Theodor's birth mother years earlier. Would Onofre lose Caroline and his children too? The uncertainty they all lived with daily would consume them if they let it. Theodor brushed aside

---

* Ephesians 6:5, 7.
† 1 Thessalonians 5:18.

those thoughts. How glad he was to have the hope and understanding of the future that the Bible gave.

"Being faithful to God is the only thing that really matters," Onofre continued. "Remember what Jesus said, 'In the world ye shall have tribulation: but be of good cheer; I have overcome the world.' "*

Theodor nodded. The sun was nearly overhead, and his stomach rumbled. It was hard to keep up this kind of work with only their prison breakfast to fuel them. He wondered what, if anything, their lunch would be.

Eventually, the farmer gave the call for lunch, and the guards escorted the tired prisoners to the farmhouse. The prisoners scooted around a large table piled with steaming food, a welcome change from the dry bread they were given at the prison every day. Before the farmer allowed the prisoners to dig in, he flagged Onofre's attention. News about Theodor and his father had, by now, spread throughout the prison, and also to the farm—that they were in prison for their faith.

"Would you please ask God's blessing for the food?" the farmer asked.

"I'd be glad to," Onofre replied. "Let's bow our heads."

After the prayer, all the prisoners devoured with gusto the generous portions that the farmer heaped on their plates. Aside from the two weeks he had spent with the interrogator's family, Theodor had not eaten like this for several months. Theodor felt sorry for the guards standing around the table with their guns, having to eat on duty while they watched the prisoners. *We wouldn't bother them,* Theodor thought. *Too bad they can't relax too.* When his stomach was as full as it could be, Theodor eyed the leftovers regretfully, wishing there were some way to bring the leftovers back to the prison with him.

After lunch, the farmer approached the guard in command.

---

* John 16:33.

"We still have much work to do," the farmer told the guard. "But I do not need all these men to finish the job. Just give me two men, and that will be sufficient."

"No problem," said the guard.

"Could you please give me those two men?" the farmer asked, pointing at Theodor and Onofre, "I've seen how quickly and how well they work. Just give me one guard to watch them."

The commanding officer waved his hand dismissively. "Those two men are Seventh-day Adventists," he said. "They do not need any guard to watch over them."

"What!" exclaimed the farmer.

"They will not go anywhere after work but back to the prison," the guard continued.

"But how will they get there?" the farmer asked.

"There's a bus stop at the end of your driveway," the guard said. "That same bus goes by the prison. Just give the prisoners their bus fare and a note asking the bus driver to drop them off at the prison gate."

The farmer looked incredulous. "All right," he agreed. Theodor, too, was surprised.

Back at work that afternoon, Theodor and Onofre enjoyed complete freedom to talk as they finished harvesting the rest of the potatoes. Afterward, they cleaned up the field, covering up the big pile of potatoes for the winter.

"Come inside for dinner," the farmer invited the prisoners after they had finished. "I don't want to send you back hungry."

"Thank you," responded Onofre and Theodor gratefully.

"Would you give the prayer for dinner?" the farmer asked Onofre again when it was time to eat.

This time, Onofre prayed not only for a blessing on the meal but also for the farmer's family and for their salvation. No one had ever prayed for the farmer and his family before, and this prayer made quite an impact on them. At the dinner table, they extensively questioned Onofre and Theodor about their faith. There was so much that the family wanted to know about God and His plan for them and so little time to talk about it.

Dark rain clouds filled the evening sky as Theodor and Onofre said Goodbye to the farmer and his wife. The couple walked with the prisoners the distance from the farmhouse to the edge of the driveway. As Theodor headed down the long dirt road, he turned for one last glimpse of the farm. The couple stood watching them, a wistful look on their faces, and the farmer's wife wiping tears from her eyes with her apron.

Local villagers waiting for the bus already loitered around the small bus stop at the end of the road. Seeing the two prisoners in their grungy garb approaching, they shrank back, eyes suspicious and fearful. Theodor and Onofre, in prison uniforms with large numbers printed on their backs, scraggly beards, and unkempt hair, were a sight the locals didn't see every day. Where was their guard? Were they escaping? But why would prisoners escape on a bus? Were they dangerous? The two men could read the questions in their worried eyes.

"Don't worry. We are not escaping," Onofre said before anyone could run for the police. "The prison authorities sent us to this farmer to help harvest his potatoes," he waved his hand back at the farm. "Now we're just going back home to the prison." A murmur of surprise rolled through the waiting passengers.

"Why are you in prison?" someone asked suspiciously.

"Well, we are Seventh-day Adventists," Onofre explained, "and we take our Bible very seriously. There's a part where it says, 'Remember the Sabbath day to keep it holy.' So we obey God instead of man, and when we refused to work on Saturday, the biblical Sabbath, they put us in prison." The fear in the villagers' eyes turned to amazement.

The bus arrived, and all the passengers boarded. Theodor and Onofre stepped onto the bus, paid their fare, and handed the bus driver the note from the farmer. The driver, reading the note, raised his eyebrows in surprise then motioned the prisoners to sit down.

The passengers currently riding in the bus edged away in their seats from the two men in prison uniforms. "Who are those men?" they murmured among themselves.

"They're OK," reassured the people who had boarded with the pair at the bus stop. "They're not escaping. They're in prison for their religious beliefs, and after helping out our neighbor with his crops, they're returning to the prison."

"Seriously? How surprising."

"How do we really know they're not escaping?" asked one passenger. "I've got to see this."

Theodor heard the whispers of the passengers around them. He couldn't help but smile. The temptation of escaping had entered his mind, but he knew it wasn't right. He remembered the conversation he had had with his father in the field. He and Onofre had been called to the prison for a reason, and they would honor the prison guard's trust. Besides, they had no reason to run and hide. God was with them.

Theodor looked out at the darkening sky as scattered raindrops began splashing against the window. He was glad that the farmer's crops were all gathered in on time. Glad to have a full stomach. Glad for the chance to talk with his father again. And over all this thankfulness, he was glad that they had had another chance to witness for Jesus.

A few more stops, a few more passengers entering and staring at the prisoners in shock, a few more explanations from the other passengers, a few more exclamations from amazed travelers, and finally the driver pulled the bus to a stop at the prison gate. All eyes were on Onofre and Theodor, following their every move.

The driver opened the bus door, and Theodor and Onofre stood up, smiled at the passengers, thanked the driver, and stepped out. The bus door closed behind them, but the bus did not move. All the passengers, including the driver, turned and watched to see where the prisoners would go. Would they indeed go right back to the prison like they had said?

Sure enough, Theodor and Onofre walked up to the prison gate and knocked; the guard opened it and let the two prisoners in. They were "home."

As the prison was made for criminals and lawbreakers, and Onofre and Theodor had proven to be neither, the authorities finally decided there was no point in keeping them there any longer. After four months of imprisonment, the good news came.

"You're free to go," the prison guards told Onofre and Theodor. The Pawluks said farewell to the rest of the inmates whom they had gotten to know. Many sad faces, including some of the prison officials, said Goodbye to Theodor and Onofre for the last time.

As father and son left the prison and headed home, dressed once again in civilian clothes, Theodor recalled the words of the angel, "Don't be afraid. The Lord with be with you." He quietly thanked the Lord for not only being with them, but also for protecting them from mistreatment during their prison term.

* — * — * — *

Following their release from Zwickau Prison, Theodor and his father enjoyed relaxing with their family for a few days before being reassigned to a different factory. At the new factory they had much more freedom on the Sabbath day than they had had before. Knowing that Theodor and Onofre would not work on the Sabbath, the factory superintendents tried to accommodate them in advance. On Saturdays, Onofre and Theodor were reassigned to the area of the automated machines. Here they were given the freedom to visit or observe the Sabbath as they wished. If a machine needed adjustment, they were to call a service tech rather than attempt the work themselves. Though it wasn't the same as being in church, Onofre and Theodor appreciated their supervisors' efforts to respect Onofre and Theodor's choice not to work on Sabbath.

"An inspector from the Gestapo is coming to our factory today," the foreman announced one morning, startling the workers and unsettling everyone. Visits from the Gestapo always spelled trouble. The dreaded visitor made his rounds. Finally a secretary came down from the main office to Theodor's unit.

"We have the Gestapo officer upstairs. He wants to see Theodor Pawluk."

Theodor stifled a groan. *Not again,* he thought. Leaving his work assignment, he followed the secretary to the office. Not knowing what to expect, he was thoroughly surprised to see the Gestapo interrogator from Zwickau Prison.

"Theodor!" greeted the officer warmly. "I'm so glad to see you." He put his arm around Theodor and gave him a shoulder hug. "How have you been?"

They chatted together for quite a while. Had the interrogator actually missed his and his father's presence in the prison?

"I'll visit you again," he promised.

The days of the Third Reich were numbered, however, and the man never made a second visit. Germany was rapidly losing the war. The Pawluks' new employment ended when the factory closed. The supply of raw material previously imported from Austria was no longer available due to a large part of that country now being occupied by the Russian army. Theodor, Onofre, and the rest of the family stayed home, concerned about what would happen to them when the Soviets arrived. No German citizen would be safe from the coming invaders, and the Pawluks' change of citizenship now branded them as traitors, no matter where they were from.

One day the local German police department called Theodor on the phone.

"We have some work for you to do," they told him. "Dress in black, if possible, and report at the station tomorrow morning by seven o'clock."

Theodor obeyed. He had no other choice. Wearing all black, he showed up at the station, apprehensive and on time.

When he reported in, to his horror, the police slipped a four-inch-wide red band, with a black swastika emblazoned on it, onto his arm. To Theodor, the symbol may as well have been a scorpion. Then they handed him a rifle with ammunition and sent him to stand guard over twenty Russian prisoners of war. The Soviet prisoners were digging on the *Panzersperre* tank barrier, a deep ditch in the highway designed to prevent the Russian tanks from going through.

From the moment he saw the prisoners' hardened faces and tough demeanors and heard their familiar Ukrainian speech, he knew he was in trouble. These twenty men were experienced war veterans. Theodor would be no match for them. Furthermore, this place was on a road deep in the forest with no one around but them and Theodor. If they discovered that Theodor was also Ukrainian, speaking the same language, he was certain they would gang up to overpower him. One against twenty would be no contest, his rifle notwithstanding.

"Do you have any cigarettes and matches," one of them asked Theodor in Ukrainian. No response. The men tried again in German. Theodor lowered his rifle and glared at the prisoner, pressing his lips tightly together, motioning for him to get back to work and to keep away. Already they were trying to get close to him. He dreaded the thought of pulling the trigger. How could he, in good conscience, kill another man?

"Easy," said the prisoner in Ukrainian, backing up. "Just checking." Theodor gave no hint of understanding. He just frowned sternly at them all, pointing his rifle. He must keep them at a distance until a replacement guard arrived.

The moments ticked by slowly as Theodor guarded the men, who constantly watched for a weakness in Theodor—one slip from him, one relaxed moment, one distraction was all these men needed to take him down, and that would be his end. Six miserable hours later, the German prison truck brought someone to relieve him; Theodor's nightmare was over.

Another one was soon to begin. Nine months after Theodor and his father's release from prison, the Third Reich surrendered unconditionally. Most of the German people, indoctrinated in the belief of their Aryan superiority, could hardly believe the news. To them it was the end of the world, especially for Nazi party members and those who had held official positions in the Third Reich. Thousands of German people committed suicide. One of these, the local policeman, who thirteen months earlier had arrested Theodor and his father at their home, hung himself in the city park.

Theodor thought of all the people with whom he and Onofre had come into contact during his imprisonment: the interrogator and his family, some of the Gestapo officers who worked for their release, the people on the train who witnessed their arrest, the people on the bus who heard of their faith and their loyalty to God's commandments, and especially the farmer's family for whom Theodor and his father had worked while prisoners. He hoped that they would recall their conversation about the Lord and His desire to save them all.

In Theodor's area, the war ended on May 7, 1945. Three and a half million German people who had lived in Sudetenland underwent vast economic changes. The new Czech government took away all their property and shipped the people, virtually empty-handed, to West Germany to rebuild their lives. More than seven million Germans lost their lives in that war,* but for the people of Eastern Europe, including Theodor's family, the trouble was only beginning.

---

* Total deaths of World War II are estimated at seventy-two million people—7,503,000 of these were Germans. "World War II Casualties." Wikipedia, http://en.wikipedia.org/World_War_II_casualties. (Accessed August 2007.)

Chapter 11

At the Yalta Conference held during February 1945, the Western Allies handed over Eastern Europe to "Uncle Joe" Stalin, as they called him. Eastern Europe included the Pawluk's homeland, the Ukraine. It also included their new homeland, East Germany. The Axis defeat meant that all this territory and its people were now under Soviet rule.

"We have to get the children out of Mährisch Trübau before the soldiers get here," said Onofre. "This place is soon going to be filled with Russian soldiers. There might be a military confrontation with them around."

"The German authorities say all military-aged men have to stay put," said Theodor. The thought of waiting for the Russians after escaping from them made him more than uneasy, but he didn't have a choice. Neither did Slawko.

"Because your mother is forty miles away at a hospital with little Thomas, I'm the one who will have to evacuate the rest of the children," Onofre explained. "The authorities have exempted me from the travel ban, or I would stay with you."

"We'll see you later then," said Theodor, not knowing any better.

On the dreadful morning of May 7, 1945, Mährisch Trübau was overrun with Soviet soldiers. The first item on the Soviets' agenda was to search for all German soldiers who had not openly surrendered to them, who had instead put away their uniforms, pretending to be innocent civilians. Forming themselves into small squads, the Soviets searched through every house in the city. If they found any German man of military age, they shot him on the spot, no questions asked.

Theodor, twenty-one years old, could easily be taken for one of the German soldiers hiding in civilian clothing. His brother Slawko was eighteen. Huddled in the front room of their barracks, a low light burning overhead, Theodor and Slawko heard the screaming begin. Gunfire, wails, and shouts echoed through the evening air. Hoping for the best and praying for protection, Theodor and Slawko sat in their chairs, frozen with terror. There was no place to go, no place to hide.

"Should we lock the door?" Slawko asked.

"They'll just break it down," said Theodor. "There's no point."

Immediately after it became dark, one of the firing squads burst into Theodor's barracks. Assuming that Theodor had been a German soldier, one of the Russians raised his gun to fire. Theodor closed his eyes, waiting for the end. *God help us,* he prayed.

Just then, another soldier grabbed the first one's arm. "Wait," he interrupted. "Don't shoot yet. I want to talk to him." The solder lowered his rifle, while the other soldier turned to Theodor.

"Who are you?" he asked,

"I'm a Ukrainian factory worker, not a German soldier," Theodor answered in Ukrainian, "and this is my younger brother." Miraculously believing Theodor's explanation, the soldiers left Theodor and Slawko alone, stalking back out of the barracks.

"Thank You, Lord," Theodor prayed, still trembling and shaking.

Theodor and his brother tried to sleep, but while they covered their ears under their blankets, they couldn't block out the yelling, screaming, crying, and calling for help—help that would never come. The night outside had become a living hell. Gunfire and brutal violence—beyond control—filled the darkness.

Another knock at the door sent Theodor into a panic. He forced himself to answer the door. A Ukrainian neighbor stood there, his face ashen.

"Come translate," he said, pulling on Theodor's arm. Theodor followed him and then wished he hadn't. A woman was lying on the ground with two dozen Russians waiting in line to rape her. She was crying and talking wildly in German. Theodor was forced to translate. Then, through blinding tears, he ran back to his barracks.

Less than an hour or so later, a second firing squad burst through the door. Without so much as a "Who are you?" the frenzied gunmen simply aimed their guns to fire at Theodor.

A huge explosion immediately outside rocked the barracks. Startled, the squad looked at each other and scrambled out of the room to see what had happened, leaving Theodor standing there, petrified with fear, expecting them to return and finish him off. Slawko, equally frozen in terror, cringed in his chair, hands over his ears, his eyes tightly shut. The soldiers did not return.

A little while later, Theodor gathered his courage and stepped outside to see the remains of the big explosion that had just saved their lives. To his amazement, no trace of any explosion whatsoever could he find. His heart filled anew with wonder. Remembering Psalm 70, he quoted quietly. " 'Make haste, O God, to deliver me; make haste to help me, O Lord. Let them be ashamed and confounded that seek after my soul: let them be turned backward, and put to confusion, that desire my hurt.'* Thank You. Thank You!"

Again the Lord had preserved his life, and Theodor praised Him from the bottom of his heart.

---

* Psalm 70:1, 2.

Toward 4:00 A.M., the army activity outside seemed to be winding down. Theodor and Slawko were hungry, nervous, and exhausted.

"Let's go into the other room and try to get some sleep before we collapse," Theodor suggested, heading for the bunks. As Slawko got up to follow, the sound of heavy footsteps at the door again made their blood chill.

"It's the Russians again," whispered Slawko. It was no use running. Theodor and his brother simply turned to face their fate. Again Theodor prayed silently for help.

A third firing squad looking for German soldiers, threw open the door, as a Soviet giant stomped into the room. His buddies blocked the doorway.

"My rifle does not understand," he yelled in Russian. "It shoots." He laughed. Swinging his rifle, he hit Theodor with the shaft of his gun, slamming him into the wall. Flipping the rifle into shooting position, the soldier raised his gun to fire.

It was too much for Slawko. He fell to the floor, unconscious. Slawko's eyes rolled back in his head, and his white face looked pathetic. He lay motionless. Startled and spooked, the Russian giant lowered his rifle. Strangely, he backed out of the room, pushing his way past his watching companions, who then turned and followed him.

"Slawko. Slawko," Theodor called him, shaking his brother's limp form. No response. Theodor went to the water jug and poured cold water over Slawko's head. Still nothing. *How long until he wakes up?* Theodor began to wonder after a few minutes had passed. *What should I do?*

In desperation, Theodor slung his brother over his shoulder and lugged him to the next-door neighbor's house. He knocked and waited, and when he realized the neighbor would not open the door, he carried Slawko to the second neighbor's doorstep. She was a nurse, so maybe she could help. The nurse opened the door, letting Theodor step inside.

Raucous laughter filled his ears. A dozen high-ranking Russian officers surrounded the neighbor's table, all drinking and celebrating the victory over Germany. Instinctively, Theodor knew that she was entertaining to escape the mass raping, and by hosting them, she hoped to avoid abuse.

"I need help," Theodor told her, shifting his brother from one shoulder to the other, trying to ignore the officers.

Seeing Theodor with Slawko on his shoulder, the Russians leaped to their feet, their guns pointing at the pair.

"What have you done to him?" one of them shouted.

"I didn't do anything. He just became frightened and fainted. I don't know how to revive him," Theodor explained, unable to tell them why Slawko got scared in the first place.

"Yeah, right," an officer said. "What really happened?" The other officers jested and threatened, their mocking voices grating Theodor's already-frayed nerves.

"Let him be," said the nurse in Russian. "I'll take a look at the boy in the other room. If he's only fainted, I know how to bring him around." Quieting the Russian officers, she led Theodor, still carrying Slawko's limp form, to the other room. Theodor laid him on the bed, and the nurse cared for Slawko until he regained consciousness.

Thanking the woman profusely, Theodor led his brother outside and back to their barracks. Exhausted, the two brothers fell asleep in their bunks.

That dreadful night of May 7, 1945, when God spared his life three times from the firing squads, seared itself on Theodor's memory. " 'Oh LORD my God, I cried unto thee, . . .' " he prayed the next morning, reading a praise from David. " 'O LORD, thou hast brought up my soul from the grave: thou hast kept me alive, that I should not go down to the pit.' "*

The search for former German soldiers in Theodor's town ended, but the raping of the German women and the looting continued for

---

* Psalm 30:2, 3.

three terrifying days. Stalin had given the Red Army permission to do all the evil they wanted for three days.

In fear of the Russians, the German families grouped themselves together, two or three families to a house. They had to display a white flag—usually a towel, a ripped up sheet, or a white shirt—as a sign of their surrender. The Communists entered every house where the Germans displayed the white flag, plundering the homes. The soldiers took away anything they could find—watches, cameras, jewelry, bicycles, and all kinds of clothing. They even took the shoes off the people's feet.

When the Russians troops had finally moved on, Onofre returned with the children to wait for their mother's return.

"I hate the Soviet regime," said Theodor vehemently to his father. "I'm not going to stay by this system. I have to get away from it."

"Now Theodor," gently lectured Onofre. "The Bible says we need to support the government and obey the laws. We are to 'render therefore unto Caesar the things which are Caesar's,' remember?* You can wait it out. Nothing is forever."

"I know," muttered Theodor. "But after what I've seen and already gone through, it will be the last of me if I have to endure it much longer."

Onofre shook his head sadly. "This world is not our home," he reminded Theodor. "No place will ever be perfect. We are looking forward to 'a city which hath foundations, whose builder and maker is God.'† Keep your eyes above the troubles of this world."

"I'll try," said Theodor. "But if the Communists think they can make me one of them, they're wrong."

A few days after the soldiers had left, Theodor went to visit a Seventh-day Adventist family in Mährisch Trübau. The family owned a fairly large house, so they had invited their frightened

---

* Matthew 22:21.
† Hebrews 11:10.

neighbors to stay with them during the harrowing times. Shortly after he arrived, one of the German neighbors, a woman, found out that Theodor could speak German and Russian.

"Would you please come to my house with me?" she asked. "I want to make sure there are no more Russians in it right now. Maybe I can salvage some of my belongings."

The house, like all the houses left behind in the wake of the looters, was a wreck. Drawers were pulled out, and clothes and papers lay strewn across the floor. "You go first," the woman insisted as they walked through room after room. But when they came near her bedroom, she asked Theodor to wait.

"Let me go first," she said.

"Sure," replied Theodor. As he opened the door for her, she looked in and wailed. A large feather pillow had been slashed on the bed, and feathers, mixed with paper currency, lay scattered everywhere. She rushed into the room, diving for the money, scooping it up in her apron, darting and desperate. "That's *my* money," she shrieked. "Don't touch it. Don't touch it!" She screamed, scurrying around the room. Theodor watched the hysterical woman with concern. "Don't take it," she cried again, her hands full. "It's mine!"

"I'm not going to take it, don't worry, but that money isn't good anymore," he said gently, but the woman continued to gather the notes, crying bitterly. *The Bible says that where your treasure is, there your heart will be also,* Theodor thought sadly.*

All this time Theodor's mother, Caroline, had been in the hospital with little Thomas, forty miles away. When the trains returned to a normal schedule, Caroline rejoined the rest of her family alone. "He's asleep in Jesus," Caroline cried softly, hugging her family for support. "He died during the operation." The whole family grieved, comforting each other with the hope that they would see little Thomas when Jesus returns.

---

* Matthew 6:21.

Upon Caroline's return, Onofre decided to move his family out of the city permanently to avoid any more unnecessary contact with the Soviet authorities and the KGB. He found a large farm just outside the city limits the family could work. The land was actually owned by the city government, and the farmhouse seemed almost like an apartment complex, with small family units dividing it. One unit was available where the Pawluks could live. Their rent would be paid with a portion of the produce they grew.

It was no use. Avoiding the KGB was easier said than done. No matter where the Pawluks moved, the KGB kept track of them. It was still May 1945 when Slawko went out to the field one morning with a message for his brother.

"The KGB wants to see you this morning at eleven o'clock," he told Theodor. "At the police station. The message just came to the farm."

"No!" Theodor groaned. "Not again! Do I have to see them so soon?" The thought of being questioned by the KGB filled him with dread. From the KGB he could expect anything—mind games, torture, imprisonment, deportation, death. Where could he ever escape from them? *Why do the police always call me and not my father?* he wondered, sighing. Regardless, he must go to the lions' den. Asking God's help, Theodor mustered his courage and walked to his eleven o'clock appointment.

Thirty people, probably all Soviet deserters as he had been, loitered anxiously in the hallway of the police station. There was no waiting room, so all the people either stood or sat on the hallway floor. Theodor found a place to sit against the wall and slumped down to wait his turn. If all these people in line were waiting ahead of him, what hope did he have to get this over with quickly?

It was nearly eleven. A KGB interrogator opened the door to his office and surveyed the waiting people. Theodor straightened, looked the man in the eye, and forced an innocent smile to his face. This was not a time to show fear. Staring back through him, but returning no smile, the officer looked once more up and down the hallway at the people. Then he walked out of his office door and disappeared through another door.

The first door opened again, and a man, his questioning completed, staggered out. Unable to hide his emotions, tears streamed from his red face. Fear throttled Theodor and he sat up, alarmed.

"What happened?" someone asked. "How did they treat you in there?" The distraught man only shook his head and brushed past the concerned people, exiting the police station. Again, the KGB officer stepped out into the hallway, scanning the waiting group. Again, Theodor sat up and smiled. The white clock at the end of the hall read eleven. Would he be next? No. Another name was called. Theodor sunk back in his position to wait again.

There was no question in his mind as to what the KGB would ask him. All the escapees now waiting in the hall had one thing in common; they had all run away from the Soviets, and now the Russians had recaptured them. Yet it was this that the waiting people could not admit—that they were deserters. If they did, the Soviets would either send them to Siberia or execute them on the spot. Just how would he answer the questions? He mulled the possibilities over and over in his mind, not coming to a conclusion. There was nothing to do but to pray and hope that somehow God would deliver him from the KGB.

The hours ticked by, but still Theodor was not summoned. Another person left the office, hands covering his face. Rushing down the hall, he, too, ignored the waiting crowd's questions. As each person left the office crying and distraught, the people remaining in the hall grew more and more frightened. Name after name was called. Even people who had arrived at the station long after Theodor were eventually called in, but still no one summoned Theodor. The interrogator continued to step out of his office, scan the hallway, and enter through another door. And always, Theodor straightened, looked him in the eye, and smiled.

Six o'clock the hallway clock now read. The waiting grew un-bearable. Could the questioning be any worse than this wait? *I just want to get it over with,* Theodor fumed. The hallway now was nearly empty. A woman exited the KGB office, her face wet with tears, white with anguish. Another name was called.

Did they forget about me? he wondered. *Maybe they will let me go without any questioning after all.* Theodor had plenty of time to toy with this unlikely hope, but he doubted it could be as easy as that. The KGB was relentless. The poker-faced interrogator had again stepped into the hallway. Theodor was now one of only two detainees left to be called. Outwardly composed, he plastered a smile on his face, looking the officer directly in the eye. The other person was called.

Alone with his thoughts and the ticking clock, Theodor pon-dered the rumbling of his empty stomach. Now 7:00 P.M., it had been a long time since breakfast.

"Theodor Pawluk."

Now more curious, desperate, and hungry than scared, Theodor walked briskly into the office.

One interrogator stood behind a desk; the other officer walked over and stood beside the first.

"Please sit down," the interrogator invited, politely waving Theodor to the seat on the opposite side of the desk. As he sat down, they sat also. Theodor acknowledged their courtesy with a nod, and smiled. Respectful and attentive, he waited for the inter-rogation to begin.

The minutes passed.

The KGB officers sat in silence across from Theodor, just staring at him. Theodor returned their gaze.

More minutes passed. The silence roared in his ears.

What's going on here? wondered Theodor, his own eyebrows arched as he contemplated the inscrutable faces of his interrogators. *Was this how they had treated the others?* A guilty conscience could be devastating under circumstances like these. *Was this how most of them had finally broken down and lost their self-control?* His own endurance was slowly stretching like a rubber band as the minutes ticked by.

My conscience is clear. I don't have to look away from you, Theodor thought, continuing to study their faces. Time passed slowly. Realizing his stamina was about to snap, Theodor breathed a silent prayer and smiled again. He had to say something.

"Why have you called me here?" Theodor asked, keeping his voice even and calm.

"We just want to visit with you," one officer said and nothing more. Theodor realized the issue would not go away.

"Well, what do you want to talk about?" he pressed. Silence.

"Would you be interested in knowing why we left our home in the Soviet Union during the German occupation and went to Germany?" Theodor asked candidly.

The officer nodded, "That might be an interesting subject."

"Well, it's simple. My stepmother's name is Miller," Theodor began, "so the name was supposedly either German or Jewish. The Nazis insisted we register as one or the other. If we did not register as German, we would end up in a concentration camp like the Jews. So, in order to escape the concentration camp, we registered as German citizens." That was the truth. As Theodor had nothing more to add, he waited.

The interrogating officer stretched back in his chair, his eyes lifted in thought. "Your testimony sounds good," he said. Then he leaned forward, thumping his hand on the table. "Tell you what. We will give you an opportunity to prove your loyalty to the Soviet Union."

"How's that?" Theodor asked.

"Isn't it true that you can speak many languages: Russian, German, Polish, Ukrainian, and Czechoslovakian, right?" A creepy feeling crawled down Theodor's spine. *If they knew all this about him, how long had they been watching him?*

"Yes," Theodor answered. "That is true."

"You can be a big help to us," the officer said. "There are people among those nationalities living here that do not feel about the Soviet government as you and we do. We would like to know who they are."

"Oh?"

"In exchange for your freedom," the man continued, "we are enlisting you as a spy for the KGB."

Theodor involuntarily widened his eyes, but he kept his voice quiet. "What?"

"Your job is to have conversations with those people and to find out from them how they feel about the Soviet system," the officer explained. "If any make derogatory statements about the Soviet government, you write those statements down. Get the names of the people, the place, and the time, and bring all this information to us."

Theodor's stomach was churning.

"Do you think you can help us?"

"Well," Theodor said, stunned. There was no way he would ever be a spy, especially for the Soviets. "This is a job that I—"

"Listen, Mr. Pawluk," the interrogator interrupted, his smile now sinister, "if you will be nice to us, we will be nice to you."

. . . *Cannot do.* Theodor finished the thought in his head, stunned and upset.

The interrogator stood up, the same artificial smile on his face. "We will meet you here in our office twice every week."

Theodor also stood up, wanting to protest, but afraid.

"Oh yes," the officer added. "Do not tell anyone about our offer, OK? Not even members of your family." He held out his hand.

Theodor had no choice but to shake it. The other officer stood and shook his hand as well, then motioned him toward the door.

"We'll see you next week," they said, ushering him out.

The spring sun was low on the horizon, and its fading light filtered through the high windows as he walked down the now empty hall, his footsteps echoing.

Do not tell anyone about our plan, the man's forbidding words stalked him, an ominous threat.

"No! I cannot do this," Theodor whispered, opening the door into the fresh air of evening. A restless anger churned inside him, and he broke into a run in the general direction of home but not caring where he went.

"Is this the help I get?" Theodor asked, throwing his question to the twilight sky. "Must I now send others to their exile or to their death?" His own forced smile and friendly nature had betrayed him. And who would suspect?

Down the quiet streets Theodor raced, trying to shake his rage, trying to escape the truth, relentless and cruel, that he was trapped. "If the Communists think they can make me one of them, they're wrong," his words sworn not long before to his father returned to mock him.

"I am a spy," he whispered, laughing bitterly. The job description nearly turned his stomach. Feeling dirty, used, and a complete fraud, he repeated to himself, "I'm a spy."

So it was that in May of 1945, Theodor became an undercover agent for the KGB.

"What happened during your interview?" his parents asked him anxiously that evening when he returned home late. "You look as if you don't feel well."

"They made me wait all day," Theodor explained evasively. "I'm starving." He dipped his spoon into the bowl of soup his mother had placed in front of him.

"What did they ask you?" Onofre inquired.

"They didn't. They just stared at me for the longest time, trying to break me into some sort of confession or into losing control. Finally, I just started a conversation with them. I asked if they wanted to know why our family had left the Ukraine for Germany."

"Did you tell them?"

Theodor took a bite of bread and butter. "Yes. I told them the truth."

"And then what?"

"They believed me. We talked a bit more after that, and then they let me go." He finished his bowl of soup and asked for a refill.

"Just like that?" Caroline asked suspiciously. Theodor was acting slightly odd.

"It wasn't fun," Theodor replied, between bites of bread. He related all that had happened in the hallway, trying to think of other details with which to distract them.

"Well, praise the Lord!" his parents finally said, when they could extract nothing more of concern. "I can't believe they just let you go, let us go, for that matter, so easily. It's a real miracle."

"Yes," said Theodor. "It's hard to believe. I'm really tired. I think I'll go to bed now." Usually quite communicative, Theodor resisted the urge to tell them everything. This was a burden he must carry alone. They would be so disappointed in him.

As he thought of what would happen to anyone whom he turned over to the KGB, Theodor could hardly stand it. He just couldn't betray innocent people. Because he had to meet with the officers twice a week, Theodor had to report something. There was much civil unrest and civilian uprisings right after the war, so Theodor dutifully reported these to the KGB—but his reports were lacking anything of substance or information implicating any people with direct personal involvement. Although he knew his real job was to report those individuals who made derogatory remarks against the Soviet system, Theodor refused.

After three months of receiving Theodor's innocuous information, the KGB realized that Theodor was not fully cooperating with them. Their genial, friendly behavior toward him began to change.

"What names do you have for us today?" the interrogator asked.

Theodor shook his head. "I overheard a man in the bus today complaining about the transit system to his seatmate, but before I could get more details about him, both men got off the bus."

"Did you follow them?"

"I wasn't able to. They got off so quickly, and then they disappeared into the crowd."

"No names? No addresses?"

"Not this time, but I'll keep working on it." Theodor remained polite and vague. The interrogator pursed his lips. His icy stare chilled Theodor, but Theodor had nothing else to offer.

"That's what you said last week."

"I'm just telling you what I hear."

"Maybe you need to get out more," the interrogator said curtly. "A young man like you should be having many social interactions."

"Yes, sir," Theodor said.

The officer leaned forward, a menacing look in his eye. "Don't trifle with us, Theodor."

"No, sir. I'll try to have something next time to report."

"I hope so," the KGB officer said ominously. "I hope we did not misjudge your loyalty to the Union."

My end is near, Theodor said to himself when he left the office.

It was Friday, the day of preparation for the Sabbath. Usually he felt a lift of joy as he anticipated the day of rest to come. But now all he felt was dread.

I can't stand this tension much longer, Theodor thought. *If I don't give them someone's name next week, I will be punished.* He sighed. Wouldn't it be easier to simply drop a name? He wasn't the one sending the person to exile or death, after all. Surely there was someone out there he didn't care for very much. Did it have to be this hard? For the first time, Theodor felt sympathy for a traitor, but he shook his head.

If it must be someone's life, it may as well be mine, he resolved. *I just can't turn anyone in.* Deliberating as he walked, he mulled over a plan of action. The July sunshine warmed his shoulders, and he savored the smell coming from a nearby bakery.

"I've got to take the first step," he decided. "I should have done this long before now." He cringed at his cowardice.

He knew now what he would do. He would go back to their office and tell them that, in all good conscience, he could not carry out this assignment. That was all. He would be either executed or banished to Siberia, of that he was certain, but there was no other way.

Swallowing his terror at the thought, Theodor quickened his pace. It was a relief to have made the decision. Before he made that final move, however, he wanted to tell his parents. He would tell them everything about his secret assignment and his decision. Then he would say Goodbye.

That Friday evening his mother put out the white Sabbath tablecloth as usual and lit the candles. After worship that evening, when the younger children were in bed, Theodor asked for a private talk with his parents. Gathering around the hearth, Theodor sat down with them, hating to break the news or their hearts.

"Remember when I had the meeting with the KGB in May?" Theodor asked. "I didn't tell you everything."

"You did seem disturbed," said Onofre, "but you insisted that everything went fine."

"Well, it didn't. They made me an undercover agent."

Caroline straightened in her chair. "A spy?"

"Yes. For the KGB," he said wryly.

"What!" exclaimed Onofre. "You? I don't believe it."

"Believe it, Father. Your own flesh and blood," Theodor said. It was a relief to come clean.

"How could you do this?" Caroline asked, not wanting to believe. "Theodor, how could you?"

"I couldn't and I can't," Theodor said. "That's why I'm telling you. Spying was forced on me against my will. I wasn't allowed to say anything to anyone, not even you. But now it doesn't matter."

Caroline clasped her hands in distress. "It doesn't matter?"

"How many people have you reported?" Onofre asked, interrupting.

"Nobody," Theodor said. "That's the good part." Onofre exhaled in relief. "The information I've been giving them has only been vague: a riot here, an uprising there, generalities. Nothing specific."

"But that's not good enough for them, is it?" Caroline asked, also relieved.

"No."

"And you've carried this secret alone for three months?" Onofre asked.

"Yes," Theodor said, looking at the fire. "I just can't do it anymore. They're getting suspicious. I think their patience is almost gone. If I don't give them specific names by our next meeting, I'm dead anyway. So I'm going to make the decision first, before they have the chance to make it for me."

"What are you going to do?" Caroline asked.

"I'm going to go to them and resign. Of course, you know what that will mean."

Caroline covered her face with her hands, unable to hold back a sob. Onofre squeezed his eyes closed in grief.

"I just wanted to tell you goodbye," Theodor said, choking up. "Who knows? Maybe they'll just send me to Siberia."

"And when are you going to tell them?" Caroline said, wiping her eyes.

"I thought about going tonight," Theodor said. "I just want to get this over—"

"Tonight!" Onofre exclaimed.

"But I think I'd like to enjoy one last Sabbath with you and the family." Theodor exhaled slowly. "So many times I've faced death or disaster unexpectedly. I didn't have time to think about it then. How ironic that now I've got to make the choice on my own schedule."

Onofre nodded. "But God has always delivered you. If He chooses, He still will. He is the only one who can help you." Caroline couldn't hold back her tears.

"I know," said Theodor. "I trust Him, and I know that hurting and betraying others isn't in His plan for me."

"Before you go see them, we will have a session of fasting and prayer tomorrow," Onofre announced. "We will ask God to help us."

All through the next day, the entire family fasted, prayed, and read their Bibles. Theodor meditated on the twenty-third psalm, one of his favorites: "Yea, though I walk through the valley of the shadow of death, I will fear no evil: for thou art with me."* Theodor sighed. The Bible also said, "Call upon me in the day of trouble: I will deliver thee."†

He remembered the countless times God had delivered him and his family before. He remembered the supernatural visitor encouraging him in the prison. Yet, why was it always so hard to trust? Where again was this perfect peace God has promised? Why, again, did he feel the terrors of the unknown and the crush of fear? God was with him, he knew, whatever happened. He just wished to be delivered from the power of fear.

"Even Jesus' disciples were scared in the storm on Galilee,"§ Onofre reminded his son. "And He was in the boat with them the entire time. Fear is built into our nature."

"I know. I just wish I could face whatever happens with peace," Theodor said.

"You can," Onofre said. "If God allows something to happen to you, we know that He allowed it for some reason. You can trust Him. I think that has to be a mental decision, even when your heart betrays you. Remember, God says that He 'is greater than our hearts.' "**

"That's fortunate," said Theodor. "Because I don't know if I can stand it."

---

* Psalm 23:4.
† Psalm 50:15.
§ See Matthew 8:23–27.
** 1 John 3:20.

Caroline reached over to hug him. "I know, Theodor," she said, tears in her eyes. "Sometimes I don't know if I can stand another loss either. This is a world of pain, but we have the assurance that we can do everything through Him who gives us strength."*

Theodor nodded, a lump filling his throat. Little Thomas's empty place in the family was a reminder of an all-too-recent loss.

"Jesus is in the boat, Theo," his father said. "He's in the boat with you too."

It was a very solemn Sabbath day for the Pawluk family. As the sun slid behind the hills, Theodor knelt with his family one last time before going to face the KGB. He hugged his parents, brothers, and sister, kissing them goodbye.

"I'll see you in a little while," he said, experiencing the calm feeling one gets before facing the inevitable. Mustering a smile, he waved at them where they stood on the porch. Their brave smiles reflected his. He knew that it was true. One way or another, no matter what happened, he would see them again "in a little while."

---

* See Philippians 4:13.

Chapter 12

The police station that housed the KGB headquarters was only three kilometers away from Theodor's home. After the short, nerve-wracking walk, he knocked on their door, as he usually did when he came to report, but no one answered. Even though evening had come, the KGB men were always there; they preferred meeting their spies under the cover of darkness.

Oh no, thought Theodor. *Do I have to prolong this?* Both disappointed and relieved, he turned to return home, but then he stopped. "I have to go through with this," he said to himself out loud. Going back to the door, he knocked louder. Still there was no answer. Walking to another door, Theodor knocked again.

This time a policeman opened it. "Yes?" he asked. "Can I help you?"

"I have an appointment with the KGB officials, but they don't seem to be here," Theodor explained. "Do you know where I can find them?"

"Those men were just transferred to the city of Brno," the policeman said. "They're no longer here. Sorry."

"Oh. Thank you," said Theodor, stunned. The policeman went back inside, leaving Theodor on the doorstep feeling weak with amazement and relief. Joy was coursing through his body as Theodor turned back toward home. Brno was five hundred kilometers away. They would not be coming back. He could hardly wait to get home and let his family know how God had answered their prayers. "Call upon me in the day of trouble: I will deliver thee, and thou shalt glorify me."* The promise repeated like a chorus in his heart. His feet had wings.

The Pawluks knew that Theodor had been saved from certain banishment or death that night, but they were still far from being safe. It seemed that the Communists and the state security committee, the KGB, had been waiting until the war was over so that they could persecute the refugees who had escaped from them during the German occupation. They would not leave the defectors alone.

Though the Pawluks continued to hope that somehow they could remain in Sudetenland, instead of going back to Russia to be punished as traitors, their wish would not be granted.

Soon after Theodor's affiliation with the KGB ended in July of 1945, the Soviets sent a large truck with KGB personnel to the Pawluk home and arrested the entire family. The KGB truck carried the family to a prison camp in Brno, Czechoslovakia, the same city where Theodor's KGB contacts had relocated. As the family traveled the five hundred kilometers, they rejoiced that at least they were together. Though apprehensive of what the future held, they continued to trust that God would see them through this trial, as well.

After a week at the prisoner-of-war camp, the Pawluks were transferred to another prison camp in the city of Sighetu Marmatiei in Romania, near the Russian border.

"This is the last camp for all escapees," the captors informed their prisoners. "In this camp every escapee will be interrogated. The KGB will now decide your destiny and punishment."

"They can force us to go where they will," Onofre told his family. "They can choose our punishment, but they cannot choose our

---

* Psalm 50:15.

destiny. Only God can control that, and He has already told us what it is."

When it was time for Onofre to be interrogated, as head of their family, he was given the bad news. "The KGB has sentenced us to ten years in Siberia," he told his waiting wife. "Our children will be taken from us and placed in a government institution."

"No!" Daria wailed.

"No," cried Theodor's younger brothers.

Theodor clenched his fists. He hated them, those Communist fiends. And what would become of him? His father didn't say.

"We've always known this could happen," said Onofre, trying to comfort his family. "God saved us from this fate back in the Ukraine, remember?" Caroline nodded through her tears.

"But our children," she said. "The Communists will try to indoctrinate them into atheism. What if we lose them forever?"

"Oh, Mother," Daria reassured. "I'm old enough to know better."

"I know," said Caroline, "But your little brothers are so young."

"We've done our best with them," Onofre said. "We have to commit them to God, trusting them to His care and pray that we will be reunited." With heavy hearts, the Pawluk family sought comfort in each other in the brief time that they remained together.

Almost two months had passed during which the KGB had screened the prisoners, executing some and placing others on the list of offenders to be shipped to Siberia. Now, in the bright morning sun, the authorities ordered all the men in the camp to assemble on to the parade ground and line up military style. Onofre, Theodor, and Slawko stepped into line with the other men. The women and children followed the men, standing in the background, watching.

"All men twenty to twenty-five years of age take three steps forward," a sergeant commanded. Theodor stepped forward. Slawko, not yet twenty, remained behind with his father. The sergeant then ordered the young men to line up and stand at attention. Once they complied, he gave the third order.

"Right face." The young men turned toward the right. "March."

Theodor picked up his feet and marched. Suddenly he realized what was happening. The young men were leaving the prison—permanently. A burst of wailing and shouting erupted as the rest of the people realized this too.

"Don't leave us," the women and children cried. Wives tried to run after their young husbands, children ran after their fathers. "Come back," they pleaded, trying to cling to the young men. But the Communist soldiers intercepted the women and children, refusing to let them have even a final word of farewell.

Theodor's heart ached for the crying wives and children. Tears streamed down his own face. He, too, longed for one last hug, one last smile, one last word of love. But without so much as a wave, on September 26, 1945, Theodor marched out of his family's lives.

"I'll see you in a little while," he whispered. Then, raising his chin, Theodor continued down the road. "I am not going to stay in this Communist system any longer," he vowed again. "I will not be a part of their system."

Theodor knew how much he would miss his family as time went on, but he would especially miss his father. In a totalitarian system like Communism, he couldn't talk freely to just anyone. His father was one of the few he could trust. Thinking back, Theodor realized that he had now lost one of his greatest treasures—not only a father, but a best friend. With his father he could talk about anything that came to his mind. At home they had worked together on the farm, then on the weaving bench. They had traveled together to all the church meetings. They had made the long trek by horse and wagon from the Ukraine to Germany together. During Hitler's regime they shared a prison cell, and after that they had worked together in the German defense factory. Now his father and the rest of his family were gone—his parents banished to Siberia, the children to an institution—while Theodor was left alone, conscripted to the Russian army.

Theodor and the troop of young men were taken to a large military compound a half hour's march from the prison camp. At this new camp, each man was checked in and then directed to his respective unit. Theodor found himself to be a new member of the Sixteenth Battalion of the Soviet army; others were assigned to the Fourteenth.

At least the new recruits had plenty to eat. Aside from marching within the compound grounds, the new soldiers received little military training. Uniforms were scarce. If someone wished to send a picture home, he had to borrow one of the few military uniforms in the camp for the occasion. That is what Theodor did.

Writing a letter to his parents at the concentration camp, Theodor told everyone Goodbye and how much he loved them all. "I'm all right," he wrote. "Don't worry about me. Here is a picture of me in the Soviet army." He wanted to say more but knew his letters were being censored. His sister, Daria, wrote back to him. His parents, he knew, were too afraid to attempt to correspond—something worse could happen to them, or to him.

Right after the war, the Soviets were interested only in one thing—military technology and how to obtain it. The new soldiers' first task was to gather discarded military hardware scattered throughout Soviet-controlled territory, remnants from the war. It did not matter whether the items were still functional or broken. They just loaded everything onto trains to be shipped back to the Soviet Union for further analysis and study. Men in both the Sixteenth and the Fourteenth battalions worked on this project from September 1945 to the middle of December; after this, both battalions were scheduled for transfer to another location.

Despite his new occupation as a Russian soldier, Theodor had one thing that no one could ever take away—the true knowledge of God that his parents had taught him. Alone and without his family,

Theodor still felt God's presence with him. God had spared his life numerous times in the past, and he knew that God would be with him in his current difficult circumstances.

Theodor often brushed his hand over the lump hidden in his coat pocket, the small Bible his father had given him long before. He could not read it openly, or it would be taken away, but whenever he grew discouraged, Theodor sneaked into the men's restroom, locking himself inside, and opened the sacred pages. There he read the precious promises for comfort, then flushed the toilet, tucking the Bible back into his pocket. He so wished that he could attend church on Sabbath again.

Hundreds of military personnel worked with Theodor and his army mates, most of them deeply involved in promoting the Soviet agenda, a program Theodor couldn't stand. Every week, Theodor, like Onofre during the politruk lectures long before, sat through lectures condemning the practices of a free society—domestic, military, government, religious—the Soviets trying to indoctrinate the new soldiers into their "better" methods. "We are an atheistic society," the lecturers reminded everyone. "We do not promote religion. If we ever find you with any religious literature, it will be confiscated."

I know, Theodor replied silently. *Believe me, I know.* The small Bible buried in his coat pocket was his one remaining treasure. No matter how loud or often the Soviets shouted their Communist doctrines at him, the words in his little book spoke louder than they.

I have to escape. The conviction grew roots in his consciousness. *I have to get out of here.* As the days and nights passed, dreaming about escape became an obsession. Yet defecting from the Soviet army was an almost impossible undertaking. Now camped in the city of Sighetu Marmatiei, Romania, they were close to the Russian border. The last thing Theodor wanted to do was cross over into Russia. But to get out of Communist territory, he would have to hike across four countries—Romania, Hungary, Austria, and

Czechoslovakia in order to get to the American Sector in West Germany. All four borders were heavily guarded by the Soviet army. If the Soviets caught him, he would be executed.

On his military cot, covering his head with a thick army blanket, he prayed every evening and morning that the Lord would bless his dangerous plan. He just wished he didn't have to travel alone.

One day while working, Theodor overheard Ivan and Petro, who like him were from the Ukraine, discussing in low tones the possibility of defecting from the Soviet army. Theodor cautiously joined the conversation, thanking God for finding him possible traveling companions. Hidden with his secret Bible, Theodor also carried a small map of Europe. Over the next few days, their plan slowly took shape. Meanwhile, they watched and waited for a good opportunity to escape.

"The Sixteenth Battalion will be transferring to the Soviet Union," the army officials announced one morning in early December. "The Fourteenth Battalion will be transferring to Austria." Theodor, Ivan, and Petro heard the news with dismay. This development would crush their plans.

No! This can't be, Theodor protested to himself. Going to Austria would have placed him closer to freedom, but they were in the wrong battalion. Defecting from the Soviet Union itself was out of the question.

Please don't send me to the Soviet Union, Theodor prayed, pleading with God for intervention. *I just can't bear it. Please!*

The following day Theodor bought a bottle of vodka with the small amount of money he had left. Bolstering his courage, he went to visit the commanding officer.

"I'd like to be transferred to the Fourteenth Battalion," Theodor said, handing the man the bottle.

The officer stared at Theodor but accepted the bottle. Theodor held his breath.

"Nyet," the officer snapped. The word was like a bullet. "No. By now all the files have gone to Moscow. There is no way you can be

transferred now." He slipped the bottle into his desk drawer. Discussion over.

Theodor left the office in despair.

God, please help! Theodor begged. *I just can't go back to the Soviet Union. I can't!* Even though he saw no way out, Theodor continued to plead daily, constantly for help. *Don't let this happen to me, God,* he pleaded.

A few days later, still early in December, the awful announcement came. "Get up. Gather your things. We're leaving for the Soviet Union," a voice over the loudspeaker announced at three o'clock in the morning, shattering the sleep of the Sixteenth Battalion. A tombstone fell on Theodor's heart. He folded his cot, rolled up his blanket, put on his jacket, and gathered the rest of his few belongings. Trudging out in the frosty air to the train station, Theodor felt as if he were going to his own funeral. He had nothing more to say to God. It was no use to pray. They were leaving. An occasional shrill whistle from the train punctuated the sentence.

The battalion arrived at the depot, and the troops boarded cold freight cars. Theodor crawled into a spot in the corner of the car and threw down his bag. Wrapping himself in his blanket, he stretched out on the hard wooden planks and cried. Heaving muffled sobs, he shook there in the darkness. *What can God do now?*

Theodor, accustomed to taking all his problems and fears to God, didn't know what to pray anymore. This was the death of his hope, and he couldn't find an ounce of faith left in his heart. While he lay there, exhausted from crying, the train lurched forward. The *click-clack* of the wheels on the rails lulled Theodor to sleep, numb with sadness.

As morning dawned and the train continued its rhythmic progress over the tracks, a sudden whoop of joy rose up from the far end of the wagon. Another shout and then laughter. The joyful noise startled Theodor and the rest of the sleeping men awake.

"What's going on?" the groggy soldiers asked. "What's all the excitement?"

"We're going to Austria, not to Russia!"

"What?" exclaimed Theodor, thoroughly shocked.

"Look at the direction we're going," answered an excited soldier. "We're heading west!"

Sure enough. As the early morning light filled the sky, the train continued rolling west on the southern side of the Danube River.

It was a long while before the exuberance in the train car settled down. Theodor returned to his corner of the car and lay down.

God has answered my prayer in His own way, he realized. *If I had been transferred to the Fourteenth Battalion as I wanted, I would now be on my way to the Soviet Union— from where there is no return.* Again tears came to his eyes.

"Thank You, Lord," Theodor prayed, humbled with gratitude and ashamed at his lack of faith. Over and over again, he thanked God, meditating on His goodness to him. " 'As the heavens are higher than the earth, so are my ways higher than your ways, and my thoughts than your thoughts,' "* Theodor quoted to himself.

Somewhere on that railroad track heading toward Austria, Theodor finally understood, no matter what happened, God would never let him down. It was time to stop trusting himself. It was time to stop being afraid. The peace he had always longed for, the peace that passes all understanding, the peace he had never quite experienced, now nested in his heart, and he fell asleep.

————*——*

After two days of traveling, the train arrived in Budapest, Hungary. There, unexpectedly, the train was delayed for two hours. The soldiers all piled out of the train to stretch their legs, surveying the area.

Ivan and Petro approached Theodor. "This place here is as good as any for defection. Let's go. Don't go back to get your stuff."

---

* Isaiah 55:9.

"No. I must get one thing," Theodor insisted. "I'll be right back." He quickly returned to the train and picked up his Bible. He slipped it into his inner coat pocket, then as an afterthought, tucked in his shaving razor, as well. Leaving all the rest of his gear, Theodor headed back to his waiting friends. Ivan carried a small bundle under his arm.

"We're just going to buy cheese and bread," Petro told the officers they passed on their way out of the train depot.

"Do you have Hungarian currency?" Theodor asked him as they walked on unchallenged.

"Of course not," said Petro.

"Good thing we don't have our uniforms yet," Ivan chuckled. "Can you imagine how hard it would be to lose three military uniforms and find civilian clothes for all of us?"

"We're lucky," Petro agreed.

To Theodor, luck had nothing to do with it. "Praise the Lord," he said, ignoring Petro's snort. If Theodor was going to escape from the Communists, he certainly was not about to pretend that he believed in their philosophy.

And so their journey began—trekking through the farmlands of Hungary, crawling across the Austrian border, narrowly escaping recapture by the Soviets in Vienna. Abandoning Petro to a mental breakdown on the streets of Vienna, Theodor and Ivan had had to continue on alone. Miraculously they had crossed the Danube River, and now, after the mad tramp for freedom, the pair had stopped to clean up and shave in the barn of a little farm on the outskirts of the city.

* — * — * — *

While the Russian soldiers searched the perimeters of the house and barn, Theodor and Ivan stood frozen, but unable to hide. A flashback of facing the firing squad that dark night in Germany flowed through his consciousness. But in the wake of that memory came his newly acquired peace. Under the scrutiny of the soldier's eyes, Theodor pleaded for the shelter of the Most High, the only cover that could help him.

It was enough.

The officer's eyes scanned the recesses of the barn but passed unseeing over the two fugitives, standing in plain sight.

"They're not here," the soldier yelled, turning away from the two men directly in front of him. Angry and disappointed, the four soldiers returned to their jeep and sped away. The drone of the engine soon faded into the distance.

Theodor sank to his knees, while Ivan slumped against the wall.

" 'O God the Lord, the strength of my salvation,' " whispered Theodor. " 'Thou has covered my head in the day of battle.' "* Ivan crossed himself. He, too, was silent with his head bowed. Theodor and Ivan quickly finished shaving and crept out of the barn. They still had to put many more kilometers behind them before stopping to rest that night.

"On to Czechoslovakia," Ivan said, trudging beside Theodor. A quiet rural road stretched out in front of them. "One more Communist country to travel through."

"The American Sector of West Germany is just on the other side, but it feels so far away," Theodor replied.

"Another illegal crossing," Ivan murmured. "How are we going to pass this one?"

"Just like all the others," Theodor reassured, "but we're going to have to be even more careful than before. Only side roads from now on."

"You're right," Ivan sighed. "No more highways." He shifted the little bundle in his arms.

By now both men were weak and exhausted. "We can't go on without food," Theodor said finally. "My energy is gone. We're going to have to ask some farmer for bread."

Ivan agreed. "I hope the farmers here are friendly." The pair took

---

* Psalm 140:7.

a chance, walking up to a lonely farmhouse. The Austrian country folk, they discovered, detested the Communists, wanting the invaders out of their country. When Theodor and Ivan would tell the farm families of their escape, the people felt sorry for them and wanted to help. No need for fear here.

One time, stepping out of a field they had just crossed, they met a farmer, riding home after his day's work.

"May we have a ride in your wagon?" the fugitives asked.

"Sure. Hop on up," the farmer said, slowing to a stop. Theodor and Ivan jumped in. The farmer's wife sat in the back of the wagon too. The woman had strange yellow skin. Theodor and Ivan sat next to her in the wagon as they bumped along.

"My wife is sick with hepatitis," the farmer explained.

"I'm so sorry," Theodor said, sympathetically. He didn't know anything about the disease, but it didn't sound good.

"So who are you fellows, and where are you going?" the farmer asked. Finding sympathetic ears, Theodor told the man and his wife everything. The farmer and his wife were so moved by the story that they gave Theodor and Ivan all the food they could carry.

Many weeks had passed since Theodor and Ivan had first started their journey. Finally reaching the Czechoslovakian border, they scoured the Austrian side for some time, trying to figure out how and where to cross the border. Finishing off the last of their provisions from the farmer's wagon, Theodor and Ivan again went to a farmhouse near the border. Theodor went up to the door alone, while Ivan sat and rested.

"May I have a glass of milk?" Theodor asked the farmer's wife when she came to the door.

She took one look at him. "Of course," she said, compassion in her voice. "Just a moment."

"There are two of us," Theodor continued.

"I'll bring two," she said and disappeared into the house.

"Where did you come from?" the woman asked while the men drank the fresh milk. Theodor told their sad tale.

"Why don't you come inside and stay with us overnight?" she invited.

"That would be wonderful. Thank you," Theodor and Ivan replied. Grateful for a roof over their heads, Theodor also hoped he could get more information on how to cross the border. After a while, the farmer, with his teenage daughter, came home from working the fields. The farmer's wife introduced the two visitors to her husband.

"Good evening, Mr. Miller," Theodor and Ivan greeted their host. Then they were introduced to the couple's daughter, Mary.

"Nice to meet you," Theodor said to the girl with the pretty blond hair and sparkling blue eyes. She blushed and smiled.

"Why don't you go wash up before dinner?" suggested Mr. Miller to Theodor and Ivan. He showed them where to get cleaned up, and after that the three men sat and talked together, waiting for the evening meal. Theodor and Ivan could hardly endure the wait. This would be their first hot meal in more than two weeks. The food was served, and the young men struggled to use table manners instead of simply devouring the home-cooked food. The farmer and his wife were gracious hosts, treating Theodor and Ivan as honored guests.

Mary smiled often, expressing sympathy and hanging onto Theodor's every word. After the meal the Millers and the tired fugitives lingered around the table, talking late into the evening. Though Ivan was more reserved, Theodor was open about his identity. Digging into his sturdy knee-high boots, he pulled out pictures of his family that he had hidden in between the double leather. The Millers asked many questions about his life and background. It was far different from the lives they knew.

In the course of the evening's conversation, the farmer excused himself from the kitchen for a few minutes, along with his wife and daughter. Ivan moved to a chair by the fireplace, nodding intermittently in his exhaustion.

"We've got to get some sleep," Ivan said. "And we still need to come up with a plan for crossing the border."

"I know," Theodor agreed, stretching his feet out under the table. "But we can make a plan in the morning. I'm enjoying talking with these folks. They seem so interested in hearing about us."

"About you, you mean," Ivan chuckled. "Have you seen how that girl follows your every word? I think she's fallen in love."

"Don't be ridiculous," Theodor snorted. "I'm a fugitive, running for my life."

"She thinks you're handsome," Ivan teased.

"Stop it," said Theodor, blushing slightly. It was pleasant, after all, to have a girl's attention. He hadn't been around any young women for a long time.

"I wonder why they're taking so long," Ivan said. "Just give me a place to lie down."

Just then Mr. Miller and his family returned from another room. The farmer took his chair across the table from Theodor, his wife and Mary returning to their seats, as well.

"Thank you for your hospitality," Theodor began. "Would you mind showing us a place where we can sleep tonight?"

"Yes, in just a moment," replied the farmer. He looked intently at Theodor. "We have a proposition for you." From the floor where he lay on the rug, Ivan opened his eyes, looking at the farmer curiously; then he closed them again. Theodor tried to suppress a yawn. The farmer's daughter looked down at her lap, blushing furiously.

"A proposition?" asked Theodor.

"Our daughter loves you very much."

Theodor's eyes opened wide, as did Ivan's once again. Theodor saw Ivan suppressing a grin. Speechless for the moment, Theodor said nothing.

"My wife and I are getting quite old," the farmer continued, "and we have a fairly large farm to care for. We would like to see you take it all over." He waved his hand to indicate the entire property. "You were born on a farm and have lived there all your life, therefore, we all, including our daughter, think you are the right man for us."

"Uh, what exactly are you saying?" asked Theodor, squirming. The girl looked up at him with a coquettish smile. Theodor flushed. The farmer's wife beamed at him.

"We'd like you to become our son-in-law," the farmer said bluntly. Ivan coughed, stifling laughter. Theodor stared at the farmer. The farmer, his wife, and daughter all stared back expectantly. *They want an answer right now?* Theodor thought, flustered. He opened his mouth but could make no reply. *It's hard to say No, especially to these people who have been so nice to me.*

"I need a little bit of time to think it over," Theodor said finally. Ivan sat up on the rug and looked at Theodor, his mouth agape. Theodor ignored him.

"That's all right, son. You go to bed and think it over," the farmer said. "And let's see tomorrow morning what you come up with. Mary will show you where you will sleep."

Mary led the two men to a loft in the barn. As the girl handed them blankets, he noticed how pretty she really was. Mary smiled at him and then left without saying a word. Theodor gulped. Why did she have to make it harder for him?

As he spread out his blanket, Theodor's mind raced wildly. *I wish I could talk to my parents,* he thought, *or even just someone from my church. This is such a big decision.* Theodor checked himself. Was he really considering this offer? The thought of good food, comfortable work, and a woman's companionship were more tempting to him than he had realized.

"I told you so," Ivan said.

"Leave me alone," said Theodor, grinning. "It's a little embarrassing."

"Don't stay awake too long thinking about it," Ivan replied, laughing. "We have a big day tomorrow. Unless you take them up on the offer."

Theodor stared up at the rafters. He closed his eyes and dreamed of golden hair.

Chapter 13

Theodor woke the next morning with winter sunlight streaming through a knothole in the barn wall. Feeling warm and cozy under his blanket, he dreaded the thought of getting up and facing the day. Suddenly he remembered his dilemma from the evening before. In the bright light of day, the possibility seemed almost ludicrous.

Leaning on his elbow, Theodor thumbed through his Bible. What did he really want in life? And what was God's will for him? Reading God's promises for the day, Theodor realized there were only two things he truly longed for right now. One, to be free from Communism, and two, to worship God freely again in a Seventh-day Adventist church. If he married this Austrian girl, whom he didn't even know and who did not belong to the same religious faith, would he really achieve either of these goals?

Splashing cold water on his face, Theodor groomed himself and shaved before going to talk with the farmer and his family.

"I hope you will not leave me alone," Ivan said, his tone serious, as Theodor started climbing down the ladder.

Theodor smiled. "I'll see you in the house, Ivan," he answered, ignoring the comment.

Theodor found the family waiting for him in the kitchen. His possible future in-laws received him with warmth and expectation, but from the look on Theodor's face, they suspected the answer.

"I have considered your kind proposal and feel it is too good to be true," Theodor began. "But as long as the Russians are occupying Austria, according to the law, I must register my presence here with the police. It would just be a matter of time until the Russians found me, and then all our happy dreams would be over." Mary's face fell.

"I can never forget that I am on the Soviet's most wanted list for as long as the Soviets are in power or as long as I live," Theodor continued. "If I do not register with the police and they find me at your place, they will charge you with harboring an army deserter."

"I understand," nodded the farmer, his face sad. "Say no more. We were just hoping. Please do not feel the need to hurry away. Stay with us for breakfast."

"Thank you," said Theodor, glad that the announcement was over.

Ivan appeared at the kitchen door, and the farmer's wife invited him in. He looked at Theodor, a question on his face.

"What took you so long?" Theodor asked his companion. "We've got a long way to travel today." Ivan sighed with relief.

After breakfast, the farmer's wife loaded them up with food for the journey. Mary handed Theodor a note. It was addressed to a neighbor who lived just up the road.

"Go to this address and give the man there this note," she said. "He will bring you across the Czechoslovakian border."

"Thank you for all your generosity," Theodor and Ivan both thanked the family. "We are sad that we have to leave such good people behind and go back to our dangerous way of life."

The farmer's trusted neighbor, actually an Austrian soldier, knew the area quite well. The three waited on the Austrian side of the border until it grew dark. Then, knowing where the border patrol guards worked and where the searchlights wouldn't reach them, he led them down a lonely road until they arrived at the safest crossing point.

"Good luck," the soldier told them. After thanking the man, Theodor and Ivan crawled quietly across the border into Czechoslovakia. They spent the night sleeping on the ground. As dawn peeped over the horizon, Theodor and Ivan brushed off the grass and stickers. A small town glinted in the early morning light below them. Slowly, they made their way down the hill into the sleepy village, walking along the narrow street. This was their mistake.

A villager on a bicycle soon came up behind them. "Good morning," he said as he passed.

"Good morning," they returned, thinking nothing of it. The villager rode on, but turned his head to get a second look at the two.

"We should have waited until there were more people out on the street," Theodor said regretfully. "We probably look suspicious to him."

The man on the bicycle kept looking back at them. Then he got off his bike, disappearing into a building up ahead. "You're right," said Ivan. "We're the only two out on the sidewalk right now. Let's get out of here." They were nearing the end of the street.

"Hands up!" Several Czech policemen yelled, bursting out of the building where the villager had just disappeared. They pointed guns at the pair.

Theodor and Ivan cringed and held up their hands. The officers swarmed them in seconds, arresting them on the spot. Pushing the fugitives ahead of them, the policemen took Theodor and Ivan inside their headquarters for questioning.

Theodor wasn't exactly celebrating, but he had faced so much peril before, that he felt the strange absence of fear. God had always delivered him.

I'm trusting You, Theodor prayed silently. *We need help again.* Ivan didn't look so composed.

"You are under arrest for crossing our border illegally," an officer said. "Who are you, and where did you come from?"

"Well, our train was heading to the Soviet Union," Ivan began, giving the destination they had been told. "When the train stopped at one of the stations, it was delayed for a while. We went into the town to do some shopping, and then the train left without us."

"Really?" said the questioner. "I'm having a hard time believing you. Why have you then come this far and crossed our border?"

"We didn't know what else to do but to go back to where we started our journey," Theodor continued, unfazed. "But we're short of money. Could you please give us some financial assistance?"

"Eh?" The policemen were thrown off guard. Unnerved by the unexpected welfare request, the Czech police released the two in a hurry.

Free again, Theodor and Ivan left the headquarters, a bit dazed from the twist of events, and made their way to the train station. Ivan stared at Theodor and shook his head. "Financial assistance?"

Theodor chuckled. "Well, don't we need some? How in the world are we going to get a train ticket?"

Ivan winked. He pulled out the little bundle he had toted throughout their flight.

"What do you have there?" Theodor asked. He had always wondered about the package that Ivan carried with him all this time. He had never seen him open it.

"It's a suit," said Ivan, proudly. Carefully opening the package, he shook out the rolled-up coat and pants.

"Nice!" exclaimed Theodor, examining the outfit with a tailor's eye. "Can you sell it?"

"That's what I've been hoping to do," Ivan said. "And I think now is the time."

He approached a group of men working on a project at the train station. After a bit of bargaining, Ivan successfully sold the suit for a modest price, just enough to buy two train tickets.

Ivan bought a ticket to the place where he had lived before his arrest, and Theodor bought a ticket to Mährisch Trübau.

"Thank you so much, Ivan," Theodor said. "You have been so

generous with me. Getting this ticket is a development far better than I could have imagined."

"Glad to help," Ivan responded.

It was soon time for them to part.

"I'd better board the train," Ivan said at the station. His train was leaving first.

"I'm sorry to say Goodbye," Theodor replied, giving a resolute smile. He felt a small lump in his throat. The two had gone through so many adventures together. "But I guess there is no other way." Ivan nodded.

"Why don't you give me your address," Theodor said. "I'd like to keep in touch."

Ivan gave Theodor his home address in Sudetenland. He would arrive there soon. Theodor gave him his former address in Mährisch Trübau. "Thank you for everything," Ivan said earnestly. "If it weren't for you . . ." he said, then shook his head. "Take care of yourself."

"You too." The two men thumped shoulders. Theodor watched his friend board the train, then, sinking down on a station bench, Theodor watched the train rumble into the distance.

"Thank you for bringing those men into my life," he prayed, remembering Petro, as well. "It would have been much more difficult without them. Though I feel lost and alone now, I know You will never leave me or forsake me."

Theodor waited for the train to Mährisch Trübau, (now called Moravská Třebová), Sudetenland. As he watched the landscape blurring past the train window, he thought of the times and places where he had lived with his family the previous two years. He remembered the day the KGB broke through the door in their barracks and took everyone away. That was six months ago. Now his family was gone, but Theodor still had many acquaintances back in Mährisch Trübau. Would the Soviet authorities look for him there?

After several hours, the train pulled into the familiar city. Theodor left the station unsure of what to do or where to go next. The cold air nipped his face as he walked aimlessly down the frozen city streets.

Though it was late December, there was still no snow. Theodor shivered. He felt exhausted and tired and his head ached. *I feel like I'm getting sick,* he thought. *Great. That's the last thing I need.*

It's Christmas Eve, he suddenly remembered. *I wonder how my family is doing?* Thoughts of his parents and siblings filled Theodor with such longing that he had to fight to control his tears. To whom could he turn in this city?

"Theodor?" a deep voice called from across the street. Theodor looked up from his sad reverie.

"Mr. Orlicek!" he answered, brightening. Stanislaw Orlicek was a friend with whom he and his father had worked. He crossed to greet the family friend. After hearing of Theodor's plight, Mr. Orlicek invited him home for Christmas.

As they sat around the Christmas Eve table, Mr. Orlicek looked carefully at Theodor.

"Theo, you must have picked up yellow jaundice somewhere. You are yellow all over—your face, your eyes." Theodor touched his face, surprised.

"What?"

"Let me see your hands." Theodor held out his hands, and for the first time in a long while, really looked at his fingernails. They were a deep yellow.

"Theodor, you need bed rest immediately! If this disease is not treated, you could eventually die," Mr. Orlicek said, concern in his voice.

"What should I do?" Theodor asked, worried.

"You need to go to the hospital," answered Mr. Orlicek. "That would be the best place. But," he paused and pursed his lips, "as soon as you register there, you will be arrested. And me, too, for harboring you here." He shook his head. "That won't work."

"Where can I go?" Theodor asked, sickened inside. The last thing he wanted to do was get a friend in trouble.

"Let me think about it for a while," Mr. Orlicek said, his face thoughtful.

Meanwhile, Theodor tried to think of where he had picked up jaundice. Then he remembered. That Austrian farmer's wife riding in the back of the wagon. The farmer and his wife had felt so sorry for him and Ivan that they had given them all the food the young men could carry, food that the woman had prepared.* He remembered her strange yellow skin.

"We're going to visit my wife's parents near Kromeriz in a few days. They live deep in Czechoslovakia, on a farm outside the village of Němčice, some three hundred kilometers from here. No one would find you there. Why don't you come with us and stay on the farm with my in-laws for a few weeks? We'll see how it goes with your health. Just don't tell anyone about being a fugitive."

"Oh no," agreed Theodor. "I won't, and coming with you there would be wonderful," Theodor said. "But I really don't want to be a bother to anyone."

"They have a basement that you could stay in. You won't be in the way. In the meantime, try not to eat food that has any fat in it." Theodor nodded. He was grateful for any place to stay where he wouldn't have to keep running and hiding.

Mr. Orlicek's in-laws quarantined Theodor in their basement. While isolated there, he spent more than two weeks resting, reading his Bible, and praying. He asked God for a quick healing. With nothing but time on his hands, Theodor meditated upon all that God had done for him during the war, and most recently, during his escape. *I must be patient,* he realized. *It may take quite a while for me to recover completely.* Aside from his weakness and quarantine, Theodor was content. He had not had it so good for many months. Here he had a comfortable bed, three meals a day, and best of all, no one could find him. Every morning when he got up, he thanked God for all His blessings, and especially for his safety here.

The nights were a different story. Nearly every night, a feverish nightmare plagued him. In his illness, the peril and risks that he

---

* Infectious jaundice can be transmitted by eating contaminated food.

had faced surfaced as haunting dreams. Theodor, in subconscious torment, sweated with fear, cried, and often shouted. Would he say something in his sleep to reveal himself? Would someone discover who he really was? The thought frightened him.

Every time Theodor awoke, he thanked God that his nightmares were only that—nightmares.

During his second week in the basement, Theodor stared at his face in the little hand mirror his hosts had provided. By the dim light, he could see that the yellow in his eyes was fading. His skin gradually returned to a healthier color, and the yellow in his fingernails receded. Feeling stronger than he had in weeks, Theodor again praised God for answering his prayers, this time for healing. Soon he could leave the basement.

That presented another dilemma. What would he do next? Where could he go? Theodor wanted to flee the Communist country as soon as possible, but he knew that to make another attempt at travel right away would be foolish. He needed to lie low and attract no attention. Perhaps, now that he had recovered, he could find some light work on a farm. He hoped the authorities would not find him in such a rural area, and as he worked, he would wait for the Lord to impress him about the next step in his journey. He would need to keep moving because, sooner or later, the KGB would find his trail.

When the yellow color completely disappeared, Theodor emerged from the dark basement. With the help of Mr. Orlicek's in-laws, he found a farmer, Mr. Bernatek—the mayor of the village of Němčice—to employ him as a hired hand. Theodor took charge of Mr. Bernatek's two workhorses, feeding and cleaning them. He plowed and raked the soil, planted seeds, and harvested the man's crops.

Theodor asked to sleep in the barn. With his continuing nightmares, the last thing he needed was to be found out while he was sleeping. Sometimes he would wake in the night in a different place from where he had fallen asleep. The barn was the best place for that, he figured. He certainly didn't want to be found sleepwalking in his employer's home.

One day, Theodor discovered an old violin in the barn. He found that it played much like the mandolin he had learned as a child. In the evenings, Theodor remained a loner, reading his Bible and playing hymns on the violin. Although Mr. Bernatek and his daughters often invited Theodor to spend time with them in the farmhouse after work or to go with them to social gatherings in the town, Theodor politely refused. No one must know that he was a fugitive.

Despite Theodor's seeming social aloofness, he and Mr. Bernatek developed a good relationship with each other. One of the farmer's daughters particularly liked Theodor, flirting with him whenever possible and often giving him extra treats to eat. Theodor relished the attention. He flirted back—a little. Mr. Bernatek and his daughter were handy people to know. The interested daughter worked in her father's home office, and Theodor soon discovered that if he needed any documents—which the Czech government seemed to require for nearly anything—all Theodor had to do was ask her for a favor. She was always delighted to help Theodor. She would type up the needed document and get her father, as the mayor, to sign it. The mayor willingly obliged. He liked Theodor and approved of his daughter's interest.

"This isn't a bad arrangement at all," Theodor congratulated himself.

As Mr. Bernatek was also the richest farmer in the village, the Czech Communists who lived in the village did not like the mayor. "You must not work so late for that capitalist," they would tell Theodor when they saw him riding home from the fields late in the evening. Once, when the farmer sent Theodor to town to pick up some products for the farm, the vendors began aggressively questioning Theodor. When they started extolling the wonders of the working-class paradise, Theodor left without buying the products.

Much to Theodor's chagrin, and unsuspecting of Theodor's fugitive status, Mr. Bernatek registered Theodor at the local police station. This was, after all, a legal requirement. Uncertain about who this stranger really was, the police required him to report to the police station every two weeks. Every time he checked in, they interrogated him.

"How did you get to Czechoslovakia?" they asked. He always told the same story.

"I was being taken by train to the Soviet Union and when the train stopped for a while, I went out to look around the area. The train left, so I came back to Czechoslovakia."

In the spring of 1946, the Yugoslavian president, Josip Broz Tito, visited Poland. While there, someone attempted to assassinate him. The Polish government, looking for a scapegoat, blamed the attempt on foreigners. President Tito, on his way home to Yugoslavia from Poland, stopped in Czechoslovakia. As a preventative measure, the Czech government locked up all foreigners for two weeks. In Němčice, the "foreigners" included Theodor, several other men, and, oddly, ten to fifteen German children who had once been active in the Hitler Youth. They were all housed together in a Czech prison.

While in the Czech prison, the police mistreated the German children aged ten to fourteen. The officers would chase the children with big sticks, and when the children hid from them under the beds, the police would roughly poke them with their sticks.

One day in the prison while Theodor was taking a shower—warm showers being one of the only perks of being in prison—another prisoner joined him in the bathroom. Something had always seemed a little odd about this man.

He's a KGB spy, suspected Theodor. *He's been planted here to get information.*

"Where are you from?" the prisoner asked.

Theodor didn't answer.

"Come on, you don't need to be afraid of me," pressed the secret agent. "I'm one of you."

I've heard that one before, Theodor thought. *Plenty of times.* Theodor wanted privacy, but the agent hung around him.

The KGB never miss any opportunity, Theodor skulked, trying to keep his space.

"Where do you live now? Where are your parents? Do you plan to stay in Czechoslovakia?" The barrage of questions flew at Theodor, but he kept his mouth shut.

"You look like a former soldier to me," the agent continued. "Have you ever served in the German army under General Vlasow?"

Theodor felt like screaming, but turned away instead. *Leave me alone,* he thought, toweling off and heading back to his cell. But the agent continued to pester. Every time Theodor showered, the agent made a beeline to harass him. Theodor surmised the agent's strategy: if the agent was annoying enough, Theodor might give an answer just to get the spy to leave him alone. This was a game Theodor refused to play.

After two weeks, President Tito left Czechoslovakia, and Theodor and the other foreigners were released from prison. Relieved, Theodor went back to work on Mr. Bernatek's farm.

"A letter for you, Theodor," Mr. Bernatek said, one afternoon after picking up the mail.

"Oh, it's from a good friend of mine," said Theodor, brightening when he read Ivan's name. He retreated to the barn to read it privately. He had written Ivan a couple times already since he had been at this farm and had received a letter from his former companion saying all was well. This time the letter chilled him.

"I've been recaptured," Ivan informed him. "The Russians are taking me back to the Soviet Union."

"No!" Theodor groaned. "Not after all this!" How his heart ached for his friend. Theodor's own nightmares intensified.

Not long after, while Theodor was working alone with the horses in a field, a stranger dressed in a leather suit rumbled up on a motorcycle. Stopping beside the nearby road, the man picked his way across the field to where Theodor plowed.

A government official, guessed Theodor, sizing up the man. *Another secret agent, no doubt. Will they ever leave me alone?*

"Are you Theodor Pawluk?" the man asked, approaching Theodor.

He knows my name. Theodor wanted to ride away, but he knew this would be too suspicious. He nodded, fear simmering in his stomach. The man asked him more questions, but all Theodor heard was gibberish. Though the man introduced himself, Theodor was deaf to anything but the pounding in his own chest.

"My name is . . . Prazan. I'm a . . . ? Theodor stared uncomprehending.

Detectives in Communist countries never give their true names, anyway. Theodor waited, mute and apprehensive. *How can I get away from this man?* But the stranger was persistent. Again and again, the man repeated to Theodor who he was. Suddenly, it sunk in.

"My name is Pastor Prazan. I'm a Seventh-day Adventist minister from Prerov. It's a city about twenty kilometers from here."

Theodor's eyes suddenly opened wide. "Oh," he said in shock.

The pastor's eyes smiled. "I was talking to your employer, Mr. Bernatek," the man said. "He told me that you were a good worker and that they all liked you very much—especially his younger daughter."

Theodor smiled, unsure of what to say.

"Your employer also told me that you have a peculiar way of life," Pastor Prazan said. "After a workday is over, you go back to your room and read a black book. You also play church hymns on your violin. This information gave me further evidence that I had found the right man."

"Found the right man?" Theodor said, cautiously.

"Yes, I got your address from an Adventist church member in Mährisch Trübau," the pastor answered. "You apparently have written to him and told him about some of your problems. He wanted me to check on you."

"Thank you," said Theodor, still wondering if he could trust this man. "How much do you know about me?"

"You defected from the Soviet army not long ago. Your parents were banished to Siberia, the police require you to check in regularly, and you're scared your terrible nightmares will give your secret away." Theodor sighed with relief. At last, here was a person he could talk to. It felt so good to be known by someone he could trust.

"It's true," he said.

"I'm concerned about you," the pastor continued. "How are you really doing?"

Theodor talked with the pastor quite some time, their conversation soon turning to spiritual things.

"Are you planning on marrying Mr. Bernatek's daughter?" Pastor Prazan asked. The question caught Theodor off guard.

"Uh, no," stammered Theodor, a bit flustered. "Why?"

"Just wondering," said the pastor. "The Bible says that believers should not be unequally yoked. You do not share the same faith."

"But I have never planned to marry her. I've just been friendly, and she does help me get important papers that I need and gets her father to sign them."

"Do you think your behavior might be leading her to wrong conclusions?" the pastor asked with parental concern. "Do you think that is fair?"

"I never thought about that," Theodor replied. He had felt slightly guilty about leading her on. "I'll try to be more reserved."

At the end of their visit, the pastor knelt down with him there in the field and prayed for Theodor.

"Please come and visit me and my church in Prerov," Pastor Prazan invited before he left. "But whatever you do, don't tell anyone in my church about your defection from the Soviet army."

"Don't worry," said Theodor. "The fewer people who know, the better."

Pastor Prazan and Theodor grew to be good friends and spent many Sabbaths together. Theodor felt fortunate to have someone with whom he could talk openly and share his woes and sorrows.

The Theodor Pawluk Story

The Czechoslovakian Communists were still suspicious about Theodor even though he punctually reported to the police every two weeks. One day the state procurator summoned him to appear before him for a special interrogation.

"I understand you are a Seventh-day Adventist, and, therefore, all your answers must be true. Who are you?" Theodor gulped, amazed at this opening.

"My name is Theodor Pawluk. I was born on February 21, 1925, in the Ukraine. During the war my parents and I were moved to Germany, where I worked until the end of the war. After the war we were taken back to the Soviet Union. On our way, we were detained in Romania. In Romania, I was enlisted in the Soviet army, and my parents were sent back to the Soviet Union. While being transported from one place to another, I failed to get back to the train on time and it left without me. Not knowing what to do, I came back to Czechoslovakia and hope to stay here. As for my citizenship, I am not sure, because before 1939 we were under the Polish system. From 1939 to June 22, 1941, we were under the Soviet system, and from June 22, 1941, to the end of the war we were under the German system." The procurator continued to ply Theodor with questions.

"What will happen to me now?" Theodor asked as the interrogation came to an end.

"Because of your citizenship complications, we must send this deposition to the Soviet Consulate, to the Polish Consulate, and to the Czech Consulate, and we will see what their conclusion will be. In three days we will have the answer for you. In the meantime, you can go back to Mr. Bernatek."

"Thank you," Theodor said. As he turned to go, his heart thudded with grim certainty. He didn't need to wonder what the Soviet Consulate would say. He already knew.

Three days was all he had.

Chapter 14

Three days. That was all the time Theodor had to get out of Czechoslovakia before the KGB would arrest him, and the clock was ticking. Riding back to the farm, he deliberated over what to do. He did not want to alarm Mr. Bernatek and tell him he was leaving because Mr. Bernatek was responsible for his having to check in with the police. That would never do. But if Theodor stayed where he was, arrest was certain.

Theodor rapped on the mayor's office door.

"Come in, Theodor," said Mr. Bernatek. "How did the interview go?"

"OK, more or less," said Theodor. "I've run into complications about my citizenship, however, and in order to stay here with you, I will need to update some documents. *An impossible task,* Theodor added silently. "If I can get your written permission to go to Prague for a few days, I can visit the consulate there to get the paperwork in order."

"Sure, sure," the mayor said. "That will be no problem. Do you have enough money for your trip?"

"Not much," said Theodor truthfully.

"Let me give you some," Mr. Bernatek said. "You'll need some for your train fare. Hurry back, though. I want you to be able to stay here with us as long as possible." Theodor knew the man meant what he said, for the mayor saw Theodor as a candidate for future son-in-law.

"Thank you very much," Theodor said. He wanted to thank him for all the time he had spent with him—Theodor had worked for the mayor from January 1946 to November, eleven months—but too much emotion would be revealing. He hated to mislead Mr. Bernatek about his true intentions, but to do otherwise would endanger Mr. Bernatek and his family. This way, the mayor could truthfully place the blame on Theodor when questioned by the KGB regarding Theodor's disappearance.

Theodor went directly to the train station. He had no time to lose. Prague was one direction, and Theodor went the other.

Theodor stopped at Pastor Prazan's house first.

"I need to get out of Czechoslovakia and into West Germany right away," he said, after telling Pastor Prazan about the interrogation. "What should I do now?"

The pastor thought a minute. "I have one member of my church who is a border-patrol officer, but he is on vacation right now and can't help us."

"Can you think of something else?" The pastor scratched his head.

"In Mährisch Trübau, where you came from, the Czech government expels hundreds of German people who live there to West Germany every Friday."

"Why is that?" Theodor asked.

"Mährisch Trübau in Sudetenland has become a part of Czechoslovakia now that the Germans lost the war," Pastor Prazan said. "The Czech government has already confiscated all the German farms and houses, and now they want the German people out for good."

"That makes sense," said Theodor.

"This might be the chance you are waiting for," Pastor Prazan continued. "Do you still have your German passport with you?"

"Yes," Theodor said. "Do you really think I have a chance to get through with the rest of the German people—and on such short notice?"

"It's worth a try," Pastor Prazan said. "I can't think of any other options."

After more discussion and prayer with the pastor's family that night, Theodor decided to take the risk. The next day he boarded the train to Sudetenland.

Arriving at the train station in Mährisch Trübau on Thursday, Theodor sought out the Czech official in charge of the deportation program. After showing his German passport, Theodor asked for permission to board with the other Germans.

"No," said the official, frowning. "You must go back to Němčice and get a release certificate from them first. There is no other way I will let you board the train."

Theodor left the station, sick and disheartened. It was now the third day. There was no use going back to Němčice now to get a release paper from the mayor. By now, his picture would be printed in the newspapers, the police and KGB would be after him.

Lord, what do I do now? he prayed. *I don't know where to go.*

The following day was Friday, the day that the Czechs would be expelling hundreds of Germans who lived in Sudetenland to West Germany. Not knowing what else to do, Theodor got himself ready to go too. He put a four-inch yellow band on his left arm, stating that he was a German citizen like the others. He carried with him the German passport that he had received from Hitler's government when he became a German citizen in 1941. Having all these, he ignored the official's instructions and reappeared at the gathering place with the rest of the German people. Maybe he could slip undetected on the train with the group. Keeping his face away from the Czech official in charge, Theodor tried to board the train. It didn't work.

"What are you doing here again?" the Czech official shouted, recognizing him. "I told you yesterday," he enunciated, "that you must go back where you came from and bring your release papers here *first!*"

"I need to leave for West Germany today, and there is no time for me to go back to my village," Theodor replied. The Germans in the train station were all watching intently. Theodor shrank back from the yelling official.

"I don't care what your reason is," the man shouted. "You cannot go to West Germany. Now get out of here."

"But sir . . ." protested Theodor. A dam of desperate tears threatened to break, but he forced them back.

"Get out of here immediately before I call the police," the official shouted. "I don't want to see you here without that release form. Move."

It was now the fourth day. Theodor was still in the country, and he didn't know what to do. "Lord, please help me," he prayed. "There is nothing too hard for You."* He stood there paralyzed in place. The people in the line behind Theodor started to murmur.

"What's going on here?" one of the Germans demanded. Standing behind Theodor with his fellow deportees, he and they had heard everything. "Why aren't you letting this man come with us?"

The Czech official frowned at the German. "That's none of your business."

"Yes, it is," he said. "This man is my friend. You have to let him come." Theodor looked at the stranger, trying to keep the shock from his face.

A woman stepped up. "He's my nephew," she stated firmly. "You can't do this to him. His family needs him. We need him. You have to let him come."

The official tried to wave the two Germans away. "No, it's not possible," the Czech growled.

A third man stepped up, and a fourth. "Let him come with us," they chorused. Theodor couldn't believe his ears. He had never met any of these people before.

---

* See Jeremiah 32:17.

"If he stays, we stay," another voice shouted. The roar of agreement from the passengers drowned out the official's objection.

"If you don't let him go, we won't go either," someone behind Theodor shouted. The rebellion was spreading.

"Go. Get on the train," the official snapped at Theodor. Theodor obediently boarded the train. The crowd cheered.

Stunned, Theodor carried his small bag onto the train and sank into a seat. *Can it really be true?* He sat there, afraid to breathe, afraid the official would change his mind and a police officer would barge in to arrest him. *Thank You, God,* he prayed, waiting for the train to move.

As the other passengers continued boarding, some thumped his shoulders in support as they passed by. The train finally started moving toward West Germany. The passengers in Theodor's car grinned at him, their camaraderie palpable. Theodor could hardly contain himself, but he still clenched his bag in his lap, afraid to let down his emotions. For years, his dream was to live in freedom, and now that dream was close to coming true.

Then, just one kilometer before the border, the train lurched to a stop. Theodor turned cold. *Could it be that the police ordered the train to stop to search for me?* he thought, terrified.

"What's wrong now?" someone asked.

"It's the final inspection," the conductor announced, moving through the aisles. "Please form a line to the office in the rear of the train. When you are called, you will step forward to have your papers inspected." Theodor again quaked with fear, but there was no way to avoid the inspection. He waited with the others.

"Next," the inspector called. The people around him were alert. It was the same story again. The official studied Theodor's German passport. Then he read Theodor's Ukrainian name. "Pawluk," he stated. "You cannot go to West Germany."

"What!" exclaimed Theodor.

"This is not a German name. You are not German. Please step off the train." The official waved him toward the door and a waiting guard. Theodor just stood there, waiting for God to intervene. What else could he do?

Again the people behind Theodor spoke up in his behalf.

"If this man cannot go with us, we are not going either," the people clamored. One after another, they tossed their documents on the inspector's desk and began stomping out of the railway car. The official was speechless at the mutiny. These Germans must be deported from Czechoslovakia. They could not stay by the border. Chagrined, the Czech official had no recourse but to give in to the people's demands.

"Alright," he said reluctantly to Theodor. "You may go on through." The man gave him an envelope containing five hundred marks,* money given to all the refugees before they crossed this border. "Now you cannot claim that we took everything away from you."

Returning to his seat, Theodor clutched the envelope, moved beyond words. *Thank You, God,* he breathed. As soon as all the passengers' documents had been verified, the train began to move, slowly gaining speed. From there, it took them only a few minutes to cross the border to the American Sector of West Germany.

As the train crossed the border, time seemed in slow motion for Theodor. The dam of tears burst and poured down his cheeks. He was free!

Free!

Theodor's head spun in a whirl of emotion—such joy, such relief, such utter elation as he had never known. To live in a free society! It was beyond his imagination.

The train unloaded its passengers in the city of Fürth, Bavaria.† As Theodor emerged from the coach and onto the station platform, the passengers who had traveled with him broke into wild applause, giving Theodor a royal welcome such as he had never seen before. They hugged and congratulated him, as though he had won a race

---

* Five hundred deutsche marks equaled approximately three hundred and fifty dollars.

† Part of West Germany.

or an election. His fellow passengers were thrilled and proud to have played such an important part in smuggling him, a stranger though he was, to freedom.

As he mingled with the people in the station, Theodor was so overwhelmed with his rescue that every time someone asked him about his dangerous past, he wept with joy. No more fear of the Soviet army, no more fear of execution and deportation to Siberia. No more hiding from the police, no more interrogations by the KGB, no more arrests, no more imprisonments, and no more placing his name on the most wanted list. It was too good to be true, a dream, but it was real. Reflecting upon incident after incident in which God had protected him, Theodor could scarcely find words to express his appreciation to God.

From now on, I will be more faithful to You than before, Theodor vowed, *in loving You, in obeying You, in serving You, and in praising You forever and ever.*

A shadow crossed his thoughts when Theodor remembered his two companions, Petro and Ivan. They had been together for almost two-thirds the distance of his escape and had endured so many dangers together. How he wished they could be with him now.

The passengers waited at the depot until another train arrived and took them to Landshut, Bavaria. There they all received new ID cards and were sent to stay with local farmers until other arrangements could be made. As soon as Theodor settled in the home of his farmer, Martin Brockmoser, Theodor wrote a letter to his former employer in Czechoslovakia.

"I'm sorry for leaving you," he wrote, "but I had to get out of Czechoslovakia in a hurry before they shipped me back to the Soviet Union. I had no time."

Mr. Bernatek replied promptly, informing Theodor that shortly after he left, the police issued a countrywide bulletin for Theodor, with a large picture of him in the newspaper, stating that he was wanted by the Soviet authorities and was "at large" in their territory.

The Lord must have hidden me again, Theodor realized. How could he repay God for His protection? He found the answer in Psalm 30:12: "O Lord my God, I will give thanks unto thee for ever."

He stayed with farmer Martin Brockmoser, his wife, and little son for five months, from September 23, 1946, until February 24, 1947. During the day Theodor and Martin worked together on the farm, and in the evening they played chess.

"Although I can use you here, I think you are an intelligent young man, and you should start pursuing your own career," Martin told Theodor one day. "You are wasting your time. Why don't you go to school or improve your tailoring? You should be pursuing your own business soon."

"Where should I start?" Theodor asked him.

"Why don't you go to your Seventh-day Adventist church in Landshut and talk to your church members about it?"

"That's a good idea," Theodor said thoughtfully, but then his face fell. "No, I cannot go to the church with these torn clothes," he said.

"Why don't you borrow my suit?" suggested the farmer.

Theodor accepted the loan gratefully and attended the church. Slipping into the pew in his borrowed suit, Theodor sighed with contentment. What a delight it was to worship in the Adventist Church again! After the service, Theodor told the members who he was and what he was looking for. They gave him the address of two Adventist Ukrainian tailors in Munich.

Returning from church that evening, Theodor told Martin what a good time he had had and of the possibility of getting work in Munich as a tailor.

"Please keep the suit until you have one of your own," Martin told Theodor. "I'm happy my suggestions are working out for you." Theodor moved to Munich, but kept in touch with Martin for many years and presented him with a fine Pawluk-tailored suit of his own.

Moving to Munich, a city with a population of over one million people, proved a lifestyle shock for Theodor. He knew a great deal about farming, but in a large city like Munich, most of the people were not interested in farming. Even so, Theodor soon was caught up in the swing of big-city life. He lived at the home of one of his employers, also Ukrainian, at the edge of the city. In the morning of every workday, he rode the streetcar to his job at the tailor shop. After work, he caught the streetcar back home. Many times those streetcars were packed with passengers, but as long as he could jump on the outside running board and hold fast with one hand to an upright post, he was safe.

With his host family, he attended a church composed of Ukrainian and Russian members. Most of the parishioners had gone through similar hardships. They exchanged stories of their experiences under Communism and of the Lord's protection.

Theodor hoped to stay in Munich permanently now that he had German citizenship. With the Nazis no longer controlling the country, Germany was a pleasant place to live. But in close succession, the two tailors he worked for received permission to immigrate, one family to America, the other family to Australia. Theodor was left without employment or housing.

Learning that Nuremberg and Fürth had tailoring jobs available, Theodor moved to Fürth. But housing in Fürth and Nuremberg was scarce due to the extensive bombing during World War II.

At the Seventh-day Adventist church in Fürth, Theodor met the Fehns, a family who had lost their only son in the Battle of Stalingrad. They invited Theodor into their home, and he stayed with them for two years and ten months. This arrangement was of some comfort to both the Fehns and to Theodor—they missed their son, he missed his family.

As Theodor gradually put the hardships of the war and his experiences behind him, the only thing that now haunted him were his nightmares, which continued for years. Theodor wrote several letters to his parents in the Soviet Union, but he never received a reply. He suspected that the KGB confiscated the letters. In the tailoring trade, Theodor soon became known for his meticulous work, and he never had trouble finding clients.

There were four Adventist churches in the Nuremberg area. The four pastors rotated churches every week so that every Sabbath of the month, the churches had a different speaker. After his times without a congregation or a pastor, Theodor especially enjoyed the treat of hearing a variety of sermons.

Following the war, and especially after the atomic bomb was invented, the general public in Germany was anxious to know what would happen to this world. "The Bible has the answer for you," the members of the Seventh-day Adventist church reassured. All throughout Germany, Adventist churches held evangelistic meetings every Sunday evening. In addition, on one Sunday a month, the members went door to door, sharing literature with every household in the city and in the surrounding villages.

Life was falling into place for Theodor. Able to worship God without government constraints, Theodor basked in his new life of peace and freedom. Except for missing his family, nothing seemed lacking. And then he saw her.

Fräulein Klara David. There were many pretty girls in the Nuremberg and Fürth churches, but Klara caught and kept his eye. Both of them were active in their church and sang in the church choir. Klara helped with the congregation's charity work, and Theodor taught a Sabbath School class and served as one of the youth leaders. As they talked and worked together, Theodor and Klara discovered many more things in common. They both had farming experience, and both had gone through sad war experiences. Both had fled from the Russians.

"She didn't run far enough, for now she is getting married to one," Theodor teased. On December 21, 1949, they were legally married in the city hall, and on January 1, the church members put on a large church wedding just for the two sweethearts.*

The newlyweds moved into an apartment and soon saved up

---

* In Germany at that time, the only legal weddings were civil weddings at the city hall.

enough money to buy a large sewing machine for their home, hoping someday to start their own business.

One evening, when Theodor came home from work, Klara met him at the door, her face lined with worry. "Two well-dressed men were just here looking for you," she said. "I've never seen them before. They said they would be back."

"They weren't church members?" Theodor asked, surprised. "The only people I know are my clients and friends from church."

"No, they weren't from this area," Klara said.

Theodor's face turned white. "The KGB," he whispered. "They're back."

"You think those two men were from the KGB?" Klara interrupted.

"Don't you remember what we heard on the radio a few weeks ago? Then we read it again in the newspaper. The Soviet secret police have been sneaking across the border from East to West Germany and have already kidnapped many Russian refugees and taken them back to the Soviet Union. They come posing as special visitors."

"But how could they possibly know where you are?" Klara asked.

He covered his face with his hands. "My letters," he said.

"What letters?"

"To my parents." Theodor groaned, sinking down on a chair.

"I don't understand."

"I've been writing letters to my parents," Theodor explained. Klara's face also turned white.

"The KGB knows where I am."

* — * — * — *

During the next few days, Klara kept the door locked. Theodor, too, watched his back on the city streets. At church that Sabbath, the head elder gave a new announcement. "The American Seventh-day Adventists will sponsor any refugee who wishes to immigrate to the United States."

Theodor nudged Klara. She looked at him, excitement in her eyes.

"Let's go," he whispered.

The two could hardly wait to register. They wanted to get as far away from the Soviets as possible. Though they had never planned to move so far, it seemed to Theodor that this was God's plan, and they followed it.

It took some time until the right sponsor could be found. During that time Theodor was very cautious about whom he met or associated with. The last thing he wanted to do was meet those two men still looking for him.

Eventually, the right sponsor turned up: Dr. H. G. Leland from La Mesa, California. Theodor and Klara went to Munich for physical exams and immigration papers. Their trip would be paid for by the World Council of Churches, an organization that coordinated the resettlement efforts of many denominations, including the Seventh-day Adventist Church.

At home, Theodor and Klara packed their belongings, giving away whatever they could not take with them. That weekend, the church gave them a special farewell.

"Don't leave," Klara's relatives begged, as did many with others, sad to see them leave. Even their conference president wrote the Pawluks a letter discouraging them from going to North America.

"Our conference president has never been hunted by the KGB," said Theodor, upon reading the letter. "I do not want to live in fear again."

On March 5, 1952, Theodor and Klara boarded the USNS *General R. M. Blatchford,* a large military ship that had been hired by the World Council of Churches to transport the refugees. The voyage lasted sixteen days. It was winter in the North Atlantic, and the wind-tossed seas were rough. Most of the time the waves washed over the deck of the ship, and the seasick passengers couldn't keep food in their stomachs. One young mother died from complications caused by the stormy weather. The ship captain asked Theodor to sew the long bag used for her watery burial.

The ship was not a luxurious liner, and the Pawluks, along with the other refugees, worked together toward the ship's upkeep. With hundreds of passengers on board, that was quite an undertaking, especially with many of the passengers seasick.

Klara, quickly recognized for her neatness, was appointed to be the head of the cleaning crew of the ship. The captain asked Theodor to work as his tailor, repairing his clothing.

When the ship passed between Florida and Cuba, the sea was calmer and the passengers more cheerful. The eager passengers began to see lights from buoys, guiding them into the New Orleans harbor. In the early morning, the USNS *General R. M. Blatchford* cast anchor in the harbor to the cheers of her rejoicing passengers. To the travel-weary lot, American soil represented freedom and was worth the hardships they had endured to get there.

As Theodor and Klara walked down the gangplank, Theodor heard his name called on the ship's loudspeaker, asking him to come back to the captain's cabin.

"Thank you for your work," the captain said, giving him thirty-five dollars for the sewing and tailoring. This was the first American money Theodor had ever seen.

Theodor and Klara continued by train to California. Their sponsor, Dr. Leland, hosted the couple in his La Mesa home. Four months later, the pair attended their first Seventh-day Adventist camp meeting in America. In the German-speaking division, an older church member introduced himself to Theodor and Klara. Discovering that Theodor had often led out in the adult Sabbath School lesson study classes in Germany, he asked, "Would you be willing to teach the Sabbath School lesson for us here at camp meeting?"

"I would be glad to," Theodor replied, accepting the challenge.

After Theodor finished teaching the class, the people swarmed around Theodor and Klara, wanting to know everything about them and where they had come from.

"We need you in our church in Los Angeles," the class members told Theodor. A few weeks later, a German pastor, William Shaeffler, visited the Pawluks in La Mesa. After talking with Dr. Leland, Pastor Shaeffler asked Theodor and Klara to put their belongings in his car. He was bringing them to Santa Monica, California, where they have lived ever since.

The years passed by quickly in their new country. At first, Theodor and Klara accepted any kind of work they could get, but as they grew financially stable, Theodor looked for tailoring work. When he discovered that tailoring in America was not as fashionable nor earned as much as in Europe, he switched to the awning trade. He worked for nine years with an awning company in Los Angeles before starting his own business. Soon his very successful business became known throughout Los Angeles County. Many famous movie stars became his customers. God was continuing to bless his endeavors.

In 1955 Klara gave birth to a son, Stephen. He was followed by daughter Ellen, five years later.

Theodor enrolled in the evening classes at the Santa Monica Community College and for three years studied English, American History, and government, preparing to take the U.S. citizenship examination. On August 20, 1958, he filed the petition for naturalization in the U.S. District Court in Los Angeles. Because Theodor had been in the Soviet army, the FBI debriefed him.

"Would you be willing to go on television to tell the American people about everything you went through with the Soviet government?" the FBI asked him when they finished the interview. Theodor declined. As soon as he had come to California, he had written many letters to the Soviet Union in search of his parents. These letters, like the letters he had written to them from Germany, were never responded to. *The KGB still knows where I live,* he realized. Knowing how the Communists had searched for, found, and assassinated General Leon Trotsky, one of their own, in Mexico, Theodor remained guarded and cautious.

On April 20, 1959, Theodor gained his United States citizenship. Now the United States of America would be his country for the rest of his life. He only wished he could have arrived here sooner, for he had found at last a place of tremendous opportunity for anyone willing to work hard. More than anything else, he exulted in the freedom he had to worship God according to his conscience. Never before had he experienced "liberty and justice for all." Freedom of speech, freedom of religion, the voting booth—with so many candidates to choose from—these were privileges he would never take for granted.

But in spite of all Theodor's business success, his growing children and loving wife, and his happiness in his new-found freedom, an unanswered question lurked, haunting him. What had become of his parents and family? He had to know. But how?

One day in January 1958, while leafing through a *Review and Herald,* the denominational magazine of his church, Theodor happened upon an article about the Adventist Church in the Ukraine. There, in the center of a picture, was his dear pastor and old friend, Stefan Smyk.

If anyone knows what happened to my parents, surely Pastor Smyk would know, Theodor thought, excitement coursing through him. For fifteen years Theodor had heard nothing from them or about them. Were they still alive? Were they back in the Ukraine again? Hope sprang in his heart.

Wasting no time, Theodor wrote a letter to the *Review,* asking how he could get in touch with Pastor Smyk. One month later, he received word from the General Conference of Seventh-day Adventists of the Northern European Division in England. He tore it open.

"If you write a letter from America to the pastor, it will put him in jeopardy with the Soviet authorities," the letter said. "Receiving a letter from any foreign country, especially the United States, would make him a marked man, as far as the Soviets are concerned. Here is the address of Pastor Andrew Maszczak, who lives in Poland. It will be less dangerous for him to receive a letter from you. Please be careful in what you write to Pastor Maszczak, and do not address him as 'pastor' because his letters will be opened by a censor."

Theodor agreed with the recommended caution and appreciated the advice. He knew that because Poland and the Soviet Union were allies, there would be no communication problem between those two countries. And, as Poland had somewhat more liberty than the Soviet Union, it would be safer to write to the pastor in Poland. As for Pastor Andrew Maszczak, Theodor knew him quite well, for it was this man, a talented preacher and editor of their denominational magazine, who had baptized him in 1938 and who had stayed often at Theodor's childhood home.

Upon learning that Theodor was alive and well in Southern California, Pastor Maszczak passed this good news along to Onofre and Caroline, who were alive and well in the Soviet Union. Soon after, Theodor received a letter and pictures from his sister, Daria.

"We are so excited to hear from you," she wrote. "We are all alive, and God has protected us, just as He took care of you. Our parents are not able to write to you because they fear the KGB."

Reading his sister's letter, tears of joy sprang to Theodor's eyes.

Thank You, Lord, he prayed. Fifteen years of hearing nothing about his family had left Theodor fearing he would never see them again this side of eternity.

Daria continued writing to Theodor for several years. His father and a younger brother each requested, through Daria, a razor knife of the type that barbers used. That was something they couldn't get in the Soviet Union. Theodor gladly sent two razor knives, which Daria said they were allowed to receive.

My father will think about me every time he shaves, Theodor reflected happily.

Daria eventually reported the sad news that their mother, Caroline, had passed away.

Then a startling invitation came, with Daria's return address. "Come home before the barbarians kill you there," she wrote.

That's not like her, Theodor thought. "The Soviets are still trying to get their hands on me," Theodor commented to Klara after reading his sister's letter. "The Soviet authorities were demanding to know from my parents where I have been during the last fifteen years. The KGB would love to bring me to my father, handcuffed, and say to him, 'Here he is.' "

Shortly afterward, another suspicious letter arrived, this time from his old friend, Mr. Orlicek, in Communist Czechoslovakia. "Come visit me here," the letter invited. Theodor again suspected the KGB was behind this.

Yet another invitation came from the Soviet Union, again via Daria. As Theodor had not responded to her other invitation, "she" sent another. "Come to Poland and meet me there," it urged.

"Daria knows that the KGB would capture me in an instant in Communist Poland," said Theodor. "She would never ask me to do this. The KGB is behind all these invitations." Daria's letters were soon cut off, and Theodor didn't hear from her for five more years.

Still longing to see his father one more time, in July of 1967, Theodor petitioned the Soviet embassy in Washington, D.C., to give Onofre permission to visit him in the United States, but the petition was refused.

If only I could see him again, Theodor wished. *And why is the KGB so persistent in trying to get their hands on me?* he wondered. *Will I ever find out?*

A silence of twenty years was his only answer.

Chapter 15

Theodor fidgeted near the customs gate at the Los Angeles International Airport, his fingers tracing the edge of a small photograph of Daria. The picture had been taken twenty-one years before, and his last memory of her spanned even further. *Will I recognize her after forty-nine years?* Klara stood beside him, her presence keeping him calm.

A newspaper photographer and three local TV cameramen waited nearby. Word had gotten out about this memorable reunion.

Slightly more than four years earlier, on August 20, 1991, the unbelievable had occurred—the Soviet Union had collapsed. Finally, Daria and Theodor could once again correspond. Theodor learned that his suspicion was correct; the KGB had, indeed, been behind those invitations to visit Communist countries. The news that his father had died just four years after Theodor had tried to get permission for Onofre to visit, broke his heart. Now he would have to wait until the resurrection for that reunion.

I'll see him again, Theodor comforted himself, looking forward with longing to the promised reunion. The thought of the years of separation between them filled him with grief. It seemed to Theodor just the other day when he and Onofre were working together in the fields, singing songs together at church, escaping to Germany as the bombs fell around them, and suffering together for their faith. It was his father's convictions and trust, after all, that had led him to his own relationship and trust in the Lord. It was Onofre's wisdom and listening ears that had supported Theodor so often through his childhood and youth. There was so much he wanted to tell his father, so much gratitude to return. *The Lord has been with us, indeed*, he thought, remembering the angel's message that fearful day in the prison.

"I wish I could see you in America," Daria had written. "It would be wonderful to see you again."

"Now *that* is a possibility," Theodor replied, excited at the thought. It took some time to get the travel documents arranged, but finally Theodor went to the travel agency and bought a fourteen-hundred-dollar roundtrip ticket for Daria from Kiev to Los Angeles. Daria, a pensioner by now, had swept the streets of Kolomeya for her living. She could never have afforded such a ticket. Theodor would regret to learn later that Daria had to sell a gold crown, pried from her mouth by a dentist, to pay the forty-two dollars for her visa.

As the passengers emerged from customs, Theodor searched the faces. He didn't recognize Daria, but she recognized him. A bundle of energy with short, gray hair and blue eyes filled with tears, rushed to greet him. Klara reached her first. Then brother and sister threw their arms around each other, crying for joy.

"How did you know it was me?" Theodor asked.

"I could recognize you anywhere," Daria exclaimed, looking past her brother's white hair and glasses into his direct brown eyes.

"I thought you would be an old babushka," Theodor teased, hugging his sixty-four-year-old sister, "but you seem to have more spunk than I do."

During the three-week visit, even though Theodor bought her new clothes, Daria continued wearing the same dress every day. Life in California was so dramatically different from what she was accustomed to. Despite excursions to Disneyland, SeaWorld, and Knott's Berry Farm, what amazed Daria the most was the freeway.

"When do the cars stop?" she once asked.

"There's no end," her brother replied.

When people would ask her, "How is life in Russia?" Daria would respond with one word: *perestroika*.

"She says they like to promise there will be improvement," Theodor said, smiling. "That means someday it's going to be good—but no one is sure just when."

Daria loved taking walks on the Santa Monica beach; this was her first time to see the ocean.

"Why do you suppose the KGB were so persistent in trying to catch me?" Theodor asked, walking on the beach with his wife and sister one evening, hoping to finally have an answer. "They were still trying to kidnap me when I lived in West Germany. Even here, after all those years, they were still trying to lure me back."

"I think one of the reasons the KGB hunted you was that for fifteen years our parents nagged the Soviet army," Daria speculated. " 'Why are all the other parents getting letters from their sons in the army except for us?' they asked."

"What did the Soviets say?"

"That you had died in battle," Daria continued. "For fifteen years we wondered whether you were alive. The KGB never let your letters through."

"Why?" Theodor knew, but he couldn't help but ask the question.

"The Soviets were very embarrassed when they finally had to admit that you had escaped to the West."

"Embarrassed?"

"Yes, they didn't want to admit that this could have happened."

"What happened to our parents in Siberia?" Theodor asked.

"Because of Father's reputation as a great Communist hero in the First World War, they let him and Mother leave Siberia after only a few years," Daria said. "We children were released from the institution too."

"Praise the Lord!" Theodor cried.

He also learned that, of his four half-brothers, two were still alive.*

"I wrote Father so many letters," said Theodor. "Why couldn't he ever write me after he learned that I was still alive and had escaped to the West?"

"Because the Soviet army told us that you had fallen in battle," Daria explained, "our parents were entitled to receive a pension in compensation. The KGB made it clear that if he wrote to you, he would lose that pension, which was their only income as he grew older," Daria said. "I was the only one who had enough 'freedom' to write you, and even then, it cost me a lot to do so. Every time I ever received a letter from you, the KGB office read your letter to me over the phone, and then I was called in for questioning. I suppose they were afraid of bad publicity abroad."

"I knew too much about the ins and outs of their system," Theodor reflected.

"Yes," Daria continued. "We lived in the Soviet Union before the war, and you worked for the collective farm, so you knew more about the system than many others. Then you served as a KGB spy, too, remember?" Daria teased.

Theodor lifted his hands in protest. How could he forget those agonizing days?

"Then you served in the Soviet army but defected," Daria continued. "The KGB figured they had good reason to keep you silent."

Theodor nodded. "I did want to write my experiences for a long time, but because many of my experiences had to do with the Soviet authorities, I was afraid to publish my story. I even turned down an invitation to speak on national television."

---

* At the time of this writing, Daria is the only surviving sibling.

Daria smiled. "But the Soviet Union has fallen. It's OK to tell the story now."

Theodor reflected on the times God had saved his life during World War II and especially during 1945, when he had been a fugitive on the Soviet military's most wanted list.

"It was not my wisdom, good planning, or good luck that delivered me from all of those circumstances," Theodor said softly. He walked along in silence, while his sister chattered on in Ukrainian. Every so often Klara would nudge him for a translation. Hearing the sweet sound of his native tongue, Theodor's mind turned back to Onofre.

Theodor remembered his father reading the twenty-third psalm, one of Theodor's favorite passages, as the family gathered around the fireplace for evening worship. His mind turned to it now, savoring the precious promises again. *"The LORD is my shepherd, I shall not be in want."* Theodor thought of the years of poverty and the shortage of food. Sometimes they had only dry bread to eat, but they had never gone without.

"He maketh me to lie down in green pastures: he leadeth me beside the still waters. He restoreth my soul." God's presence had always proved faithful, ever an oasis of calm in the desert of fear.

"He leadeth me in the paths of righteousness for his name's sake." Theodor remembered, as a child, walking with his father down the long road, holding his hand. The gentle hand of his heavenly Father was still holding his hand tightly.

"Yea, though I walk through the valley of the shadow of death, I will fear no evil: for thou art with me; thy rod and thy staff they comfort me." Theodor remembered the Jewish men, marching to their death, the cries of the dying, the sometimes unspeakable suffering and deaths he had witnessed through the years. His heart filled with pain.

"God has a plan," Onofre had always said. "This world, with its grief, will soon pass away. God will restore." Though Theodor had always wanted to be a pastor, life's road had taken him another way. But this other way had, nevertheless, been God's special way for him. His life's story, marked with persecution, hardship, and deliverance, could serve as reassurance to God's people, especially to those living at the close of time.

"Thou preparest a table before me in the presence of mine enemies: thou anointest my head with oil; my cup runneth over. Surely goodness and mercy shall follow me all the days of my life." The psalm included everything Theodor felt, encompassing all he had experienced, holding all his hope. As relentlessly as the KGB had hunted him, God's mercy and faithfulness had pursued him even more. This he never could escape.

A warm ocean breeze blew through Theodor's hair as he strolled with Klara and his long-lost sister down the Santa Monica beach, sand squishing beneath their sandals. The setting sun, dipping behind a riot of pink and purple clouds, showered them with glowing light.

Someday, rising into more glorious light, Theodor finally would tell his father all that was on his heart. Together they would kneel before their heavenly Father, expressing their gratitude and praise to the One who had given them so much—peace for this life and joy evermore. *"And I will dwell in the house of the* LORD *for ever,"* he thought, finishing the psalm.

There I will have all the time to praise Him that I need. Our short time on earth is not long enough to thank God for all His blessings and protection, he reflected, looking at the silver sunlight undulating on the tide.

Not long enough.

More About Theodor and His Family

Through the years, Theodor continued to see God's providence and lifesaving power both in his own and his family's lives. When Theodor's son, Stephen, was five months old, Stephen almost died from an intestinal obstruction. After an emergency operation and four days in the hospital, Stephen bounced back. "He is still bouncing," reports his proud father.

Stephen married Carol Shorter, and they have two children, Matthew and Katherine. Stephen has a doctor of education degree and teaches at La Sierra University. Theodor's daughter, Ellen, married a Seventh-day Adventist minister, Jan Kaatz. They have two children, Christopher and Amanda, who attend Seventh-day Adventist schools. Ellen has a master's degree and teaches elementary school in Glendale, California.

In 1990, Theodor's right hand developed carpal tunnel syndrome, refusing to open or close. As a result of a physical exam needed before a minor surgery on his thumb, they discovered Theodor had prostate cancer. The surgery to remove the cancer was a success, and Theodor praised the Lord for sparing his life yet again.

Theodor (back row left) with Ukrainian friends. 1943.

Theodor Pawluck (back row center) with other Adventist youth wearing local costumes. 1943.

Theodor in the Soviet army.
1945.

Slawko Pawluk in front of the village
Catholic church.

Onofre Pawluk

Kolomeya church members. 1947.

Theodor. 1948.

Klara. 1948.

Theodor and Klara's wedding. January 1, 1950.

Daria Ivanov and Theodor Pawluk embrace after being separated for 49 years. 1991.

If you enjoyed this exciting story, you'll want to read these other exciting stories of God's miraculous rescues.

Between Hell and High Water
Kay Kuzma and Brenda Walsh

Read the gripping accounts of people who survived the worst hurricane in U.S. history and the sorrowful stories of those who did not.

- Meet a former NFL football player as he struggles to keep his mother alive—on life support.
- Hang on with Pat as she's swept along in the violent flood, frantically grabbing on to tree branches while trying to shake off the rats clinging to her.
- Meet Red whose addictive habits had destroyed his will to live—until he starts helping those who lost everything.

These stories of life and death, hope and despair, good and evil, generosity and greed will stay with you. They will give you courage, faith, and hope as you face your own times of trouble and remind you that God is always there.
Paperback, 255 pages.
ISBN 13: 978-0-8163-2153-7   ISBN 10: 0-8163-2153-1

Escape From Saigon
Ralph S. Watts

Who lives? Who dies? More than thirty years ago, a Vietnamese conference president and his staff wrestled all night with that decision. This is the story of the dramatic evacuation of Seventh-day Adventist Vietnamese and overseas personnel as the North Vietnamese forces closed in on Saigon. Ralph S. Watts, who directed the evacuation, gives his eyewitness account of the mayhem and its impact on the church and gives information about the Seventh-day Adventist work in Vietnam today.
Paperback, 128 pages.
ISBN 13: 978-0-8163-2113-1   ISBN 10: 0-8163-2113-2